OPPOSING
VIEWPOINTS®
SERIES

The New Censorship

Other Books of Related Interest

Opposing Viewpoints Series

America's Changing Demographics
Campaign Finance
The Fifth Estate: Extreme Viewpoints from Alternative Media
Identity Politics
Party Politics
Politics and Journalism in a Post-Truth World

At Issue Series

Celebrities in Politics
Gerrymandering and Voting Districts
Partisanship
Political Corruption
Politicians on Social Media
The Politicization of the Supreme Court

Current Controversies Series

Are There Two Americas?
Attacks on Science
The Capitol Riot: Fragile Democracy
Hate Groups
Political Extremism in the United States
The Two-Party System in the United States

"Congress shall make no law ... abridging the freedom of speech, or of the press."

First Amendment to the US Constitution

The basic foundation of our democracy is the First Amendment guarantee of freedom of expression. The Opposing Viewpoints series is dedicated to the concept of this basic freedom and the idea that it is more important to practice it than to enshrine it.

OPPOSING
VIEWPOINTS®
SERIES

The New Censorship

Gary Wiener, Book Editor

GREENHAVEN
PUBLISHING

Published in 2023 by Greenhaven Publishing, LLC
29 E. 21st Street
New York, NY 10010

Articles in Greenhaven Publishing anthologies are often edited for length to meet page
requirements. In addition, original titles of these works are changed to clearly present
the main thesis and to explicitly indicate the author's opinion. Every effort is made to
ensure that Greenhaven Publishing accurately reflects the original intent of the authors.
Every effort has been made to trace the owners of the copyrighted material.

Cover image: George Sheldon/Shutterstock.com

Library of Congress Cataloging-in-Publication Data
Names: Wiener, Gary, editor.
Title: The new censorship / Gary Wiener [editor].
Description: First Edition. | New York, NY : Greenhaven Publishing, 2022. |
    Series: Opposing viewpoints | Includes bibliographical references and
    index. | Audience: Ages 15+ | Audience: Grades 10-12 | Summary:
    "Anthology of essays examining censorship in the 21st century, including
    via cancel culture and social media"-- Provided by publisher.
Identifiers: LCCN 2021055643 | ISBN 9781534508811 (library binding) | ISBN
    9781534508804 (paperback)
Subjects: LCSH: Cancel culture--United States--Juvenile literature. |
    Censorship--United States--Juvenile literature. | Social
    media--Political aspects--United States--Juvenile literature. | Academic
    freedom--United States--Juvenile literature. | LCGFT: Essays.
Classification: LCC HM1176 .N48 2022 | DDC 363.310973--dc23/eng/20211217
LC record available at https://lccn.loc.gov/2021055643

Manufactured in the United States of America

Website: http://greenhavenpublishing.com

Contents

The Importance of Opposing Viewpoints

Perhaps every generation experiences a period in time in which the populace seems especially polarized, starkly divided on the important issues of the day and gravitating toward the far ends of the political spectrum and away from a consensus-facilitating middle ground. The world that today's students are growing up in and that they will soon enter into as active and engaged citizens is deeply fragmented in just this way. Issues relating to terrorism, immigration, women's rights, minority rights, race relations, health care, taxation, wealth and poverty, the environment, policing, military intervention, the proper role of government—in some ways, perennial issues that are freshly and uniquely urgent and vital with each new generation—are currently roiling the world.

If we are to foster a knowledgeable, responsible, active, and engaged citizenry among today's youth, we must provide them with the intellectual, interpretive, and critical-thinking tools and experience necessary to make sense of the world around them and of the all-important debates and arguments that inform it. After all, the outcome of these debates will in large measure determine the future course, prospects, and outcomes of the world and its peoples, particularly its youth. If they are to become successful members of society and productive and informed citizens, students need to learn how to evaluate the strengths and weaknesses of someone else's arguments, how to sift fact from opinion and fallacy, and how to test the relative merits and validity of their own opinions against the known facts and the best possible available information. The landmark series OpposingViewpoints has been providing students with just such critical-thinking skills and exposure to the debates surrounding society's most urgent contemporary issues for many years, and it continues to serve this essential role with undiminished commitment, care, and rigor.

The key to the series's success in achieving its goal of sharpening students' critical-thinking and analytic skills resides in its title—

Opposing Viewpoints. In every intriguing, compelling, and engaging volume of this series, readers are presented with the widest possible spectrum of distinct viewpoints, expert opinions, and informed argumentation and commentary, supplied by some of today's leading academics, thinkers, analysts, politicians, policy makers, economists, activists, change agents, and advocates. Every opinion and argument anthologized here is presented objectively and accorded respect. There is no editorializing in any introductory text or in the arrangement and order of the pieces. No piece is included as a "straw man," an easy ideological target for cheap point-scoring. As wide and inclusive a range of viewpoints as possible is offered, with no privileging of one particular political ideology or cultural perspective over another. It is left to each individual reader to evaluate the relative merits of each argument—as he or she sees it, and with the use of ever-growing critical-thinking skills—and grapple with his or her own assumptions, beliefs, and perspectives to determine how convincing or successful any given argument is and how the reader's own stance on the issue may be modified or altered in response to it.

This process is facilitated and supported by volume, chapter, and selection introductions that provide readers with the essential context they need to begin engaging with the spotlighted issues, with the debates surrounding them, and with their own perhaps shifting or nascent opinions on them. In addition, guided reading and discussion questions encourage readers to determine the authors' point of view and purpose, interrogate and analyze the various arguments and their rhetoric and structure, evaluate the arguments' strengths and weaknesses, test their claims against available facts and evidence, judge the validity of the reasoning, and bring into clearer, sharper focus the reader's own beliefs and conclusions and how they may differ from or align with those in the collection or those of their classmates.

Research has shown that reading comprehension skills improve dramatically when students are provided with compelling, intriguing, and relevant "discussable" texts. The subject matter of these collections could not be more compelling, intriguing, or urgently relevant to today's students and the world they are poised to inherit. The anthologized articles and the reading and discussion questions that are included with them also provide the basis for stimulating, lively, and passionate classroom debates. Students who are compelled to anticipate objections to their own argument and identify the flaws in those of an opponent read more carefully, think more critically, and steep themselves in relevant context, facts, and information more thoroughly. In short, using discussable text of the kind provided by every single volume in the Opposing Viewpoints series encourages close reading, facilitates reading comprehension, fosters research, strengthens critical thinking, and greatly enlivens and energizes classroom discussion and participation. The entire learning process is deepened, extended, and strengthened.

For all of these reasons, Opposing Viewpoints continues to be exactly the right resource at exactly the right time—when we most need to provide readers with the critical-thinking tools and skills that will not only serve them well in school but also in their careers and their daily lives as decision-making family members, community members, and citizens. This series encourages respectful engagement with and analysis of opposing viewpoints and fosters a resulting increase in the strength and rigor of one's own opinions and stances. As such, it helps make readers "future ready," and that readiness will pay rich dividends for the readers themselves, for the citizenry, for our society, and for the world at large.

Introduction

> *"A state that seeks to control*
> *information no longer needs*
> *bureaucrats or policemen: Instead,*
> *the opponents of free speech can flood*
> *the information space with false,*
> *distracting or irrelevant information*
> *so that people have trouble*
> *understanding what is real and what*
> *is fake."*
>
> —Anne Applebaum,
> The Washington Post

Despite the United States having been founded on the principle of free speech, book banning, blacklisting, and other forms of shutting down citizens have gone on for years. Censorship is certainly not a new topic. In the past, it has been largely right-wing elements that attempted to silence those they disagreed with. In the 1950s, during McCarthyism, many left-leaning actors, writers, and performers were hauled before Congress and subsequently drummed out of the public eye. This remains an infamous period in US history.

Today, however, it is chiefly conservatives who complain about being subject to censorship. The "new censorship" refers to this twenty-first century phenomenon, where liberals have begun to "cancel," "boycott," or otherwise shun those that they disagree with. But it's not just left-leaning people who are practicing the new censorship. Conservatives are also attempting to combat ideology with which they disagree by censoring their political opponents. Witness efforts to ban books that deal with race or

LGBTQ issues and the right-wing reaction to critical race theory and the 1619 Project.

In short, this new wave of censorship can be blamed on no particular ideology or political leaning. Both conservatives and liberals have done their fair share of practicing "cancel culture" and other silencing techniques. In a country as politically divided as the United States in the twenty-first century, people seem less interested than ever in hearing what the other side has to say. Instead, any progressive idea is immediately branded as communism or socialism, and every conservative idea is labelled as racism or sexism. Some of these criticisms are warranted; many are not. Both sides have sought to refine their techniques of canceling what the other has to say, drowning out their opponent's ideas, or simply refusing to listen.

The title of a *Washington Post* opinion piece by Anne Applebaum suggests one of these new techniques. "The new censors won't delete your words—they'll drown them out," it reads. The article cites Tim Wu, a Columbia University law professor, who wrote an essay that asked, "Is the First Amendment obsolete?" According to Applebaum, "Wu pointed out that a state—or, indeed, anyone—that seeks to control information does not need bureaucrats or policemen: Instead, opponents of free speech can drown out ideas and language they don't like by using robotic tools, fake accounts, or teams of real people operating multiple accounts." Wu observed that "it is no longer speech itself that is scarce, but the attention of listeners." Common sense ideas can now be overwhelmed by an avalanche of political invective. Under Vladimir Putin, Russia has been successfully attacking democracies worldwide with an army of trolls designed to overwhelm reason, bombard gullible users with misinformation, and influence elections. Automatic software programs called "bots" enable perpetrators to blitz social media with nefarious pre-programmed information.

Not just the United States, but countries around the world have had to deal with a flood of misinformation, lies, and deception. In a country such as the United States, where freedom of speech is protected in the Bill of Rights, citizens tend to balk at the idea of censoring ideas, no matter how destructive they can be. But the First Amendment is often misinterpreted. It states that "Congress shall make no law … abridging the freedom of speech." The amendment says nothing about private enterprise. If a corporation such as Facebook or Twitter decides certain types of hate speech or health misinformation are antithetical to the public good, they are well within their rights to deal with such speech as they see fit. When social media platforms booted former president Donald Trump off their sites, it had nothing to do with the laws of American government. Instead, the bans were enacted because he had violated their terms of use. For example, Instagram states on its site, "Accounts that don't follow our Community Guidelines or Terms of Use may be disabled without warning."

Social media sites are often slow to do so, however, because, quite naturally, they depend on building the number of users in order to increase advertising and thereby increase profit. Kicking off (or turning off) too many users is not good for business. Mark Zuckerberg, CEO of Facebook, knows this only too well. For years, certain Facebook groups have been a cesspool of calls for violence, hate speech, and misinformation. Yet Zuckerberg has been loath to combat these problems with anywhere near the resources they require. In the fall of 2021, whistleblowers emerged who released evidence that Facebook was actively harming some of its users. The US Congress took an interest, holding hearings. But cleaning up a corporation the size of Facebook, which boasts a market cap of well over a trillion dollars, is no easy task, especially when its executives are resistant. Social media has become the proverbial 800-pound gorilla.

It is far easier to shut down individuals than corporations, and the new censorship has been active and growing in the early twenty-first century. Progressives, both on and off college campuses, have attacked and attempted to cancel a range of performers and speakers from right wing ideologue Milo Yiannopoulos to comedian Roseanne Barr. Conservatives are actively attempting to bring down liberal thinkers, such as the 1619 Project's Nikole Hannah-Jones. Efforts are underway in several Republican-dominated states, such as Texas, to ban books by LGBTQ and Black authors.

The new censorship would seem, therefore, to be inextricably linked with the growing partisan divide in the United States and around the world. Conservatives and liberals who formerly could hold reasonable and rational dialogues no longer seem willing to do so. Instead, the impulse is to ban the other side or shut it down. *Opposing Viewpoints: The New Censorship* presents a wide range of essays that define and debate the various modes of censorship that have recently emerged. In chapters titled "Is Cancel Culture a Threat or a Necessity?" "Is Opposition to the 1619 Project and Critical Race Theory Censorship?" "Should Social Media Be Censored?" and "Should There Be Censorship in Academics?", these essays represent voices from both conservatives and progressives, as the two ideologies vie for dominance in public discourse in the twenty-first century.

CHAPTER 1

Is Cancel Culture a Threat or a Necessity?

Chapter Preface

In November 2021, NFL quarterback Aaron Rodgers tested positive for COVID-19. Because he had misled reporters and the public by stating the previous summer that he was "immunized," when, in fact, he had not been vaccinated but had instead opted for homeopathic treatments, public backlash was immediate and harsh. Rodgers then compounded his error by going on a radio show in order to explain himself. "I realize I'm in the crosshairs of the woke mob right now," he said. "So before my final nail gets put in my cancel culture casket, I think I would like to set the record straight on so many of the blatant lies that are out there about myself."

That same day, Green Bay–based Prevea Health ended its partnership with Rodgers. He had been a spokesperson for the health organization since 2012. The canceling of Aaron Rodgers had begun, and so had the debate over its legitimacy. Some Fox News reporters praised Rodgers, commending him for doing his own research and for standing up to those fomenting fear about COVID-19. Many fans of *Jeopardy*, which Rodgers had guest-hosted the previous summer, were incensed that he had lied about his vaccine status and therefore put contestants at risk. The debate showed no sign of ending any time soon.

Rodgers is just one of many public figures whose alleged sins have had an impact on their careers. Although conservative media would have its listeners believe that cancel culture is an invention of the left, the most famous example of the practice in the US occurred during the McCarthy era of the 1950s, when alleged communists in America's entertainment era were blacklisted.

A decade later, the conservative right attempted to cancel the Beatles in the 1960s, after rock iconoclast John Lennon made the ill-advised comment that the group was "more popular than Jesus." The remark enflamed passions in the Bible Belt and resulted in boycotts, radio bans, and Beatles album bonfires. But the reality was that the Beatles were indeed so popular that they couldn't be completely canceled.

Again, in the early 2000s, country-rock darlings the Dixie Chicks ran into trouble with their own fan base of Southern conservatives after vocalist Natalie Maines criticized the US invasion of Iraq and added that "we're ashamed that the president of the United States is from Texas." The Dixie Chicks could not weather the storm Maines's remarks ignited as well as the Beatles had because they had a narrower base of fans, including fans who supported Bush and the US armed forces. The Dixie Chicks were blacklisted by thousands of radio stations.

So if it seems that the current wave of cancel culture is dominated by the political left, it must be viewed in the wake of this long history. Yet it is also true that liberals have begun to respond to speech and actions they consider offensive with a vengeance. Some of the current wave of canceled celebrities would seem appropriate. Sex offenders such as comedian Bill Cosby, movie mogul Harvey Weinstein, rapper R. Kelly, and news anchor Matt Lauer have all been driven from the mainstream. Others, such as J. K. Rowling, author of the Harry Potter series, have been subjected to lesser penalties. Rowling has been canceled by some for transphobia. The controversy started when Rowling tweeted remarks that aligned her with what is called TERFism. TERFs (trans exclusionary radical feminists) believe that transgender women aren't women and that biological sex is the only factor that determines someone's gender. Calls for boycotts of all things Harry Potter are likely to be ineffective, because, like the Beatles, Rowling and Potter are deeply ingrained in pop culture worldwide.

Another celebrity who has come under fire for his attitude toward transgender people is comedian Dave Chappelle. Chappelle was formerly a favorite of the left for his insightful satiric takes on racism, but he has become the target of a cancel culture campaign for jokes that many on the left consider inappropriate. Comedians such as Jerry Seinfeld have complained that it is difficult to tell jokes in an era of political correctness because so many topics are off limits. Seinfeld has singled out college campuses, where students, he believes, are too quick to label humor as racist or sexist. But others have argued that it's not difficult to be funny as well as respectful to marginalized groups.

All of these examples suggest that cancel culture is real but that it is not confined to either side of the political spectrum. What is clear is that today's celebrities need to watch what they say and how they say it more than ever.

> "The most common area of opposing arguments about calling out other people on social media arises from people's differing perspectives on whether people who call out others are rushing to judge or instead trying to be helpful."

Where Some See Calls for Accountability, Others See Censorship and Punishment

Emily A. Vogels, Monica Anderson, Margaret Porteus, Chris Baronavski, Sara Atske, Colleen Mcclain, Brooke Auxier, Andrew Perrin, and Meera Ramshankar

In the following viewpoint, Emily A. Vogels, Monica Anderson, Margaret Porteus, Chris Baronavski, Sara Atske, Colleen Mcclain, Brooke Auxier, Andrew Perrin, and Meera Ramshankar consider the results of polls given to Americans regarding their understanding of the term "cancel culture." It is unsurprising that opinions about the practice vary widely, especially among those who identify with political philosophies such as liberal and conservative. Conservatives, for example, are more likely to view cancel culture as censorship, while liberals often view it as a necessary way to adjust offensive speech or practices. The wide range of responses suggests that the debate over cancel culture is likely to persist for some time. The authors of this study all work for the Pew Research Center.

"Americans and 'Cancel Culture': Where Some See Calls for Accountability, Others See Censorship, Punishment," by Emily A. Vogels, Monica Anderson, Margaret Porteus, Chris Baronavski, Sara Atske, Colleen Mcclain, Brooke Auxier, Andrew Perrin, and Meera Ramshankar, Pew Research Center, May 19, 2021. Reprinted by permission.

As you read, consider the following questions:

1. What general trends does the research on cancel culture suggest?
2. What is meant by "accountability" with regard to cancel culture?
3. How do some see gray areas with regard to cancel culture?

People have challenged each other's views for much of human history. But the internet—particularly social media—has changed how, when and where these kinds of interactions occur. The number of people who can go online and call out others for their behavior or words is immense, and it's never been easier to summon groups to join the public fray.

The phrase "cancel culture" is said to have originated from a relatively obscure slang term—"cancel," referring to breaking up with someone—used in a 1980s song. This term was then referenced in film and television and later evolved and gained traction on social media. Over the past several years, cancel culture has become a deeply contested idea in the nation's political discourse. There are plenty of debates over what it is and what it means, including whether it's a way to hold people accountable, or a tactic to punish others unjustly, or a mix of both. And some argue that cancel culture doesn't even exist.

To better understand how the U.S. public views the concept of cancel culture, Pew Research Center asked Americans in September 2020 to share—in their own words—what they think the term means and, more broadly, how they feel about the act of calling out others on social media. The survey finds a public deeply divided, including over the very meaning of the phrase.

Who's Heard of "Cancel Culture"?

As is often the case when a new term enters the collective lexicon, public awareness of the phrase "cancel culture" varies—sometimes widely—across demographic groups.

Overall, 44% of Americans say they have heard at least a fair amount about the phrase, including 22% who have heard a great deal, according to the Center's survey of 10,093 U.S. adults, conducted Sept. 8–13, 2020. Still, an even larger share (56%) say they've heard nothing or not too much about it, including 38% who have heard nothing at all. (The survey was fielded before a string of recent conversations and controversies about cancel culture.)

Familiarity with the term varies with age. While 64% of adults under 30 say they have heard a great deal or fair amount about cancel culture, that share drops to 46% among those ages 30 to 49 and 34% among those 50 and older.

There are gender and educational differences as well. Men are more likely than women to be familiar with the term, as are those who have a bachelor's or advanced degree when compared with those who have lower levels of formal education

While discussions around cancel culture can be highly partisan, Democrats and Democratic-leaning independents are no more likely than Republicans and GOP-leaning independents to say they have heard at least a fair amount about the phrase (46% vs. 44%). (All references to Democrats and Republicans in this analysis include independents who lean to each party.)

When accounting for ideology, liberal Democrats and conservative Republicans are more likely to have heard at least a fair amount about cancel culture than their more moderate counterparts within each party. Liberal Democrats stand out as most likely to be familiar with the term.

How Do Americans Define "Cancel Culture"?

As part of the survey, respondents who had heard about "cancel culture" were given the chance to explain in their own words what they think the term means.

The most common responses by far centered around accountability. Some 49% of those familiar with the term said it describes actions people take to hold others accountable.

A small share who mentioned accountability in their definitions also discussed how these actions can be misplaced, ineffective or overtly cruel.

Some 14% of adults who had heard at least a fair amount about cancel culture described it as a form of censorship, such as a restriction on free speech or as history being erased.

A similar share (12%) characterized cancel culture as mean-spirited attacks used to cause others harm.

Five other distinct descriptions of the term "cancel culture" also appeared in Americans' responses: people canceling anyone they disagree with, consequences for those who have been challenged, an attack on traditional American values, a way to call out issues like racism or sexism, or a misrepresentation of people's actions. About one-in-ten or fewer described the phrase in each of these ways.

There were some notable partisan and ideological differences in what the term "cancel culture" represents. Some 36% of conservative Republicans who had heard the term described it as actions taken to hold people accountable, compared with roughly half or more of moderate or liberal Republicans (51%), conservative or moderate Democrats (54%) and liberal Democrats (59%).

Conservative Republicans who had heard of the term were more likely than other partisan and ideological groups to see cancel culture as a form of censorship. Roughly a quarter of conservative Republicans familiar with the term (26%) described it as censorship, compared with 15% of moderate or liberal Republicans and roughly one-in-ten or fewer Democrats, regardless of ideology. Conservative Republicans aware of the phrase were also more likely than other partisan and ideological groups to define cancel culture as a way for people to cancel anyone they disagree with (15% say this) or as an attack on traditional American society (13% say this).

Does Calling People Out on Social Media Represent Accountability or Unjust Punishment?

Given that cancel culture can mean different things to different people, the survey also asked about the more general act of calling out others on social media for posting content that might be considered offensive—and whether this kind of behavior is more likely to hold people accountable or punish those who don't deserve it.

Overall, 58% of U.S. adults say in general, calling out others on social media is more likely to hold people accountable, while 38% say it is more likely to punish people who don't deserve it. But views differ sharply by party. Democrats are far more likely than Republicans to say that, in general, calling people out on social media for posting offensive content holds them accountable (75% vs. 39%). Conversely, 56% of Republicans—but just 22% of Democrats—believe this type of action generally punishes people who don't deserve it.

Within each party, there are some modest differences by education level in these views. Specifically, Republicans who have a high school diploma or less education (43%) are slightly more likely than Republicans with some college (36%) or at least a bachelor's degree (37%) to say calling people out for potentially offensive posts is holding people accountable for their actions. The reverse is true among Democrats: Those with a bachelor's degree or more education are somewhat more likely than those with a high school diploma or less education to say calling out others is a form of accountability (78% vs. 70%).

Among Democrats, roughly three-quarters of those under 50 (73%) as well as those ages 50 and older (76%) say calling out others on social media is more likely to hold people accountable for their actions. At the same time, majorities of both younger and older Republicans say this action is more likely to punish people who didn't deserve it (58% and 55%, respectively).

People on both sides of the issue had an opportunity to explain why they see calling out others on social media for potentially offensive content as more likely to be either a form of accountability or punishment. We then coded these answers and grouped them into broad areas to frame the key topics of debates.

Some 17% of Americans who say that calling out others on social media holds people accountable say it can be a teaching moment that helps people learn from their mistakes and do better in the future. Among those who say calling out others unjustly punishes them, a similar share (18%) say it's because people are not taking the context of a person's post or the intentions behind it into account before confronting that person.

In all, five types of arguments most commonly stand out in people's answers. A quarter of all adults mention topics related to whether people who call out others are rushing to judge or are trying to be helpful; 14% center on whether calling out others on social media is a productive behavior or not; 10% focus on whether free speech or creating a comfortable environment online is more important; 8% address the perceived agendas of those who call out others; and 4% focus on whether speaking up is the best action to take if people find content offensive.

Are People Rushing to Judge or Trying to Be Helpful?

The most common area of opposing arguments about calling out other people on social media arises from people's differing perspectives on whether people who call out others are rushing to judge or instead trying to be helpful.

One-in-five Americans who see this type of behavior as a form of accountability point to reasons that relate to how helpful calling out others can be. For example, some explained in an open-ended question that they associate this behavior with moving toward a better society or educating others on their mistakes so they can do better in the future. Conversely, roughly a third (35%) of those who see calling out other people on social media as a form of unjust punishment cite reasons that relate to people who call out others being rash or judgmental. Some of these Americans see this kind of behavior as overreacting or unnecessarily lashing out at others without considering the context or intentions of the original poster. Others emphasize that what is considered offensive can be subjective.

Is Calling Out Others on Social Media Productive Behavior?

The second most common source of disagreement centers on the question of whether calling out others can solve anything: 13% of those who see calling out others as a form of punishment touch on this issue in explaining their opinion, as do 16% who see it as a form of accountability. Some who see calling people out as unjust punishment say it solves nothing and can actually make things worse. Others in this group question whether social media is a viable place for any productive conversations or see these platforms and their culture as inherently problematic and sometimes toxic. Conversely, there are those who see calling out others as a way to hold people accountable for what they post or to ensure that people consider the consequences of their social media posts.

Which Is More Important, Free Speech or Creating a Comfortable Environment Online?

Pew Research Center has studied the tension between free speech and feeling safe online for years, including the increasingly partisan nature of these disputes. This debate also appears in the context of calling out content on social media. Some 12% of those who see calling people out as punishment explain—in their own words—that they are in favor of free speech on social media. By comparison, 10% of those who see it in terms of accountability believe that things said in these social spaces matter, or that people should be more considerate by thinking before posting content that may be offensive or make people uncomfortable.

What's the Agenda Behind Calling Out Others Online?

Another small share of people mention the perceived agenda of those who call out other people on social media in their rationales for why calling out others is accountability or punishment. Some people who see calling out others as a form of accountability say it's a way to expose social ills such as misinformation, racism, ignorance or hate, or a way to make people face what they say online head-on by explaining themselves. In all, 8% of Americans who see calling out others as a way to hold people accountable for their actions voice these types of arguments.

Those who see calling others out as a form of punishment, by contrast, say it reflects people canceling anyone they disagree with or forcing their views on others. Some respondents feel people are trying to marginalize White voices and history. Others in this group believe that people who call out others are being disingenuous and doing so in an attempt to make themselves look good. In total, these types of arguments were raised by 9% of people who see calling out others as punishment.

Should People Speak Up if They Are Offended?

Arguments for why calling out others is accountability or punishment also involve a small but notable share who debate whether calling others out on social media is the best course of action for someone who finds a particular post offensive. Some 5% of people who see calling out others as punishment say those who find a post offensive should not engage with the post. Instead, they should take a different course of action, such as removing themselves from the situation by ignoring the post or blocking someone if they don't like what that person has to say. However, 4% of those who see calling out others as a form of accountability believe it is imperative to speak up because saying nothing changes nothing.

Beyond these five main areas of contention, some Americans see shades of gray when it comes to calling out other people on social media and say it can be difficult to classify this kind of behavior as a form of either accountability or punishment. They note that there can be great variability from case to case, and that the efficacy of this approach is by no means uniform: Sometimes those who are being called out may respond with heartfelt apologies but others may erupt in anger and frustration.

> *"Without the freedom to openly discuss ideas, make jokes, and offer opinions, we can't grow, thrive, and reach our potential as a society."*

Censorship Makes America Weaker

John Hawkins

In the following viewpoint, John Hawkins asserts that cancel culture is contributing to a lack of trust in our culture. He believes that cancel culture is forcing those who are not in the majority to self-censor, afraid that saying the wrong thing will get them silenced. Public speech is losing its meaning because people are afraid to state their opinions publicly. John Hawkins is the founder of Right Wing News and the author of 101 Things All Young Adults Should Know.

As you read, consider the following questions:

1. How does the author argue that cancel culture denies citizens freedom of speech?
2. How is the quotation by Chris Rock relevant to the author's point?
3. According to the viewpoint, how does censorship ultimately become "arbitrary"?

"Why Censorship and Cancel Culture Make America Weaker," by John Hawkns, August 4, 2021. Reprinted by permission.

I t's hard to tell whether the liberal love of censorship and cancel culture comes from sheer arrogance or the fear that the American people will reject their ideas if the other side gets a fair hearing. Perhaps it's something in-between the two … what psychologists like to call fragile high self-esteem:

> There are many kinds of high self-esteem, and in this study, we found that for those in which it is fragile and shallow it's no better than having low self-esteem. People with fragile high self-esteem compensate for their self-doubts by engaging in exaggerated tendencies to defend, protect and enhance their feelings of self-worth.

Whatever the case may be, the impulse towards censoring and canceling contrary opinions in American culture today is extraordinarily harmful. Even setting aside the fact that "freedom of speech" is such a foundational American value that it's mentioned in the First Amendment of the Constitution, there are a myriad of problems tied to or stemming directly from censorship and cancel culture.

For one thing, it's one of the many reasons why America is increasingly becoming a low-trust culture. How can I trust you if you're not free to say what you really think? More importantly, why would I trust you if you don't think I should be free to say what I really think?

It also contributes to tribalism. Because if you are not allowed to listen to me and say, "Gee, that idea you have actually makes sense," because you'll be ostracized and maybe even canceled, tribalism becomes the safe choice. It's much easier to say, "Those are bad people, and we won't even listen to them," than it is to address their ideas and in the process, start thinking or believing something that may get YOU censored or canceled. This is part of the reason our society has started to replace honesty and authenticity with outrage peddlers who specialize in getting as close as they can to the line where they'll be censored without going over it. Instead of original thinkers, we're increasingly getting people repeating bumper sticker slogans their side agrees with because at least that won't get them in trouble. It's more boring because we realize that at its core, it's safe and fake, not what anyone really thinks.

This is also why, despite our endless streams of information and entertainment, our public speech is becoming increasingly pointless. It's because of self-censorship driven by fear of being canceled. It's just like Chris Rock said:

> I see a lot of unfunny comedians, I see unfunny TV shows, I see unfunny award shows, I see unfunny movies 'cause no one's—everybody's scared to, like, you know, make a move. You know, that's not a place to be. We should have the right to fail. Because failure is a part of art. You know what I mean? It's the ultimate cancel, but now you got a place where people are scared to talk, that's not—especially in America—you're scared to talk, but that's what people want, you gotta make adjustments and, you know, let's do it.

Additionally, censorship inevitably ends up being arbitrary. White supremacists have objectionable views. Of course, so do critical race theorists, members of Black Lives Matter and the Nation of Islam, communists, socialists, anarchists, atheists, Satanists, and pretty much everyone who puts a pronoun in their bio. Do you think Donald Trump is too dangerous to be allowed to speak? Okay, but then what about the Squad, Nancy Pelosi, Bernie Sanders, and Eric Swalwell? Inevitably, the vast majority of people getting censored are just people the censors fear, dislike, or are jealous of and believe they can get away with canceling. If the social media monopolies believed they could get away with censoring the average Republican without significantly hurting their bottom line, they'd happily do it.

Of course, all of this is making our society more ignorant and mentally flabby. For example, what does it say about our society that people are apparently so incapable of refuting white supremacists or conspiracy theorists that those people have to be censored? Maybe more people should get off Twitter and try reading some books for a change and this will become less of a problem. Being exposed to the counterarguments to poorly reasoned thought is

HAS CANCEL CULTURE GONE TOO FAR?

Cancel culture is something that has taken over entertainment and media the past few years. In most cases, cancel culture starts when someone on a social media platform makes an observation of something, doesn't like it and eventually influences others to not like it. Then, a group forms to ultimately cancel—meaning to not watch, use, or support something in order to get a point across.

An example of this very recently is the Pepe Le Pew character from the Looney Tunes franchise. The character is a French skunk who flirts often with female characters and tries to kiss them; it's his schtick.

The character was fine until 2021, when a group of people told the company that owned the Looney Tunes that the character doesn't give consent and "normalizes rape culture," according to the *Washington Post*, in a March 9 article titled "How Pepe Le Pew became the latest character in the culture war."

Now, generally speaking, the character shouldn't be canceled, but for people who have dealt with assault, the character may traumatize them. It's a cartoon character and French men are known to be flirtatious and that's why the character acts the way it acts.

However, if people come together and show mass support to cancel something then there's a right to cancel that thing or idea.

Cancel culture seems to just cancel things that don't hold up in today's world. Societal norms are more consent-based now, which means some older programs may generate controversy.

Another instance of culture cancellation can be found in *Snow White*. Some people want to cancel this classic film because of the kissing scene involving Prince Charming and a lack of consent, according to *USA Today*, in a May 6 article titled " Disneyland's Snow White ride faces backlash over Prince Charming's kiss."

In reality, it doesn't make much sense to cancel because, in the story, Snow White is asleep and must be awakened by a kiss; she can't give consent to the prince who kisses her in her sleep.

The movie was made in 1937 when consent wasn't regarded much in society, but now times are different and society has evolved for the better, making consent a requirement for everything. This movie couldn't be made in 2021, but we shouldn't ruin a classic that isn't harmful or insensitive.

"Has Cancel Culture Gone Too Far?" by Cynsere Kelly, the *American River Current*, May 19, 2021.

like getting a vaccine. If you haven't heard the other side, then even something as stupid as the idea that the earth is flat can start to make sense to millions of people. If all these people are forced into dark corners of the Internet, where they mainly interact with other people that agree with them, their views will likely become more entrenched. Meanwhile, the people that are censored will appear more edgy and hip to people on the fence. "Those guys are so dangerous they had to CENSOR them!" However, if these bad actors were able to talk in public, smart people could actually refute their bad ideas publicly.

This leads us to the worst part of censorship and cancel culture. That is, contrary to what a lot of people seem to believe, no one has all the answers, which inevitably means that censorship and cancel culture often lock in bad or untrue ideas. The "experts" get it wrong all the time while culture and opinions about "the facts" change regularly. Being in favor of slavery was an unremarkable belief 220 years ago. 120 years ago, the general consensus was that women shouldn't be allowed to vote. Sixty years ago, we hadn't reached a "scientific consensus" on the idea that smoking was bad for people. Anyone who thinks they have it all figured out culturally, ethically, morally, or scientifically is not just wrong, they're ignorant. The smarter people get, the more they realize that they don't have all the answers and need to hear alternate ideas and opinions. It's hard for people to offer up those ideas and opinions when a joke tweet from 2010 can cost them their careers. Without the freedom to openly discuss ideas, make jokes, and offer opinions, we can't grow, thrive, and reach our potential as a society. To be a truly free people, we need free speech.

> *"Questioning and calling out public figures who influence and shape our world and social mores isn't being 'intolerant of opposing views,' it's merely challenging them. When you're not used to it happening, it feels like an attack."*

It's Not Cancel Culture, It's Consequences

Toula Drimonis

In the following viewpoint, Toula Drimonis discusses the consequences that are now being doled out, often to those in privileged positions who formerly were not held responsible for their speech or actions. Drimonis defends cancel culture, claiming that detractors cannot offer an example where someone who was canceled did not deserve that fate. Instead, she asserts, it is very difficult to hold those in power accountable, and she cites the Bill Cosby case as an example. For Drimonis, it is about time that "the chickens [are] coming home to roost," and that marginalized minorities have a voice in calling out insensitivities as well as crimes. Victims want to live in a world where perpetrators face consequences. Toula Drimonis is a Montreal-based writer, editor, and columnist.

"It's Not Cancel Culture, It's Consequences," by Toula Drimonis, Cult Mtl, July 14, 2020. Reprinted by permission.

As you read, consider the following questions:

1. What does the author agree with in the *Harper's* letter signed by Noam Chomsky, Margaret Atwood, and J. K. Rowling, among others?
2. Why was a performance of SLAV canceled at the Montreal Jazz Festival?
3. Why do a majority of women not report assault to authorities?

A recent *Harper's* letter in which prominent writers and thinkers of our time, like Noam Chomsky, Margaret Atwood, and J.K. Rowling, expressed concerns that "cancel culture" is stifling free speech and muzzling dissent, has sparked much debate. The letter was quickly shared by those who seem to feel that we're living in an era where accountability for your words and actions is a cruel injustice no one should ever have to suffer through.

In the letter, "cancel culture" is described as "an intolerance of opposing views, a vogue for public shaming and ostracism, and the tendency to dissolve complex policy issues in a blinding moral certainty."

There are fragments of the letter that I agree with. With the notable exceptions of hate speech or incitement to violence, my right to express myself includes my right to offend you. We need to make sure we make room for mistakes, questions, and trial and error in public conversations, so that people aren't afraid to voice their thoughts—and inevitably even change them. Most importantly, we need to be able to discern between things that are uncomfortable and things that are hateful, so we can encourage the former and eliminate the latter.

This letter, however, isn't an argument in defence of free speech; it's a plea for less accountability. The accusation of censorship is deeply insulting to activists around the world currently imprisoned, persecuted, and risking their lives for speaking out against regimes. It's also inaccurate. Questioning and calling out public figures who influence and shape our world and social mores isn't being "intolerant of opposing views," it's merely challenging them. When you're not used to it happening, it feels like an attack.

Challenging Unfair Social Structures

Another letter in response to the one published in *Harper's*, arguing that "marginalized voices have been silenced for generations in journalism, academia, and publishing," is the one that gets it right. It accurately points out that the signatories are all privileged, with massive platforms, and their fears are not centred on real repercussions of censorship, but merely a reactionary backlash to changing expectations. Like *The Beaverton* wrote in jest, "Allow me to use my nationally syndicated column to tell you how my voice is being suppressed."

I don't believe that an offensive tweet from 2014 is grounds for someone's dismissal or ostracization. People evolve and grow. But being afraid of losing your job, your byline, or a book contract because you're exposed as a racist, or a rapist, or incompetent at what you do, isn't "cancel culture," it's just boring old consequences. Are people unable to see that because the people in prominent positions are believed to be above the fray and above reproach? Do we continue to mistake talent for character?

It's true that we're living in an increasingly divisive and polarizing online world. These are unsettling times and those with the most privilege to lose will be made the most uncomfortable. In the midst of a global pandemic and an expansive Black Lives Matter movement making us cast a much-needed critical glance at every aspect of our lives, it's become undeniably clear the devastation and death of COVID-19 has affected the most marginalized in our society.

This has justifiably led to attempts to eradicate systemic racism and discrimination and revamp our institutions. Demands to defund police and reallocate funds differently—a notion that would have been until recently unheard of to a majority that hasn't been at

the receiving end of racial profiling and excessive police brutality–
is now being discussed and taken seriously in much wider circles.

In simple terms, more people are beginning to challenge the
status quo and the mainstream voices telling them their dismay
and outrage are not legitimate reactions to an unjust system, but
the reactionary and illogical outbursts of a mob out for blood.

Slowly, But Surely

Precisely two years ago, when the Montreal Jazz Festival—amidst
major protests and international criticism—decided to pull the plug
on SLAV, many Quebec pundits called it "an attack on freedom of
speech" and "censorship." The hyperbolic among them went so far
as to characterize legitimate criticism as "intellectual terrorism"
and "cultural Apartheid" refusing to understand that the festival
was facing consequences, not censorship.

Never mind that SLAV was a predominantly white show
produced by a white producer with a white entertainer front and
centre singing Black spirituals inspired by slavery. Never mind
that mainstream pundits conveniently forgot that protests and
criticism are legitimate and legal "freedom of speech," too. The
outrage it generated was deemed unjustified and hysterical by some.
"Cancel culture" was thrown around as protesters were ridiculed
and dismissed as "angry radicals."

Two years later, and while much remains to be improved on,
I doubt that a tone-deaf production like SLAV would ever be
attempted today. "The past is a foreign country, they do things
differently there," wrote author L. P. Hartley.

Progress is messy and non-linear and almost doesn't feel like
progress at all at times, but it happens. People make decisions
(intentionally or not) that are limited and framed by their privilege,
their ignorance or experience of trauma and inequality. They
get called out. They resist, they rationalize; they resent it. It's
uncomfortable to be challenged. To be told that what you're doing,
saying, or supporting is hurtful and insensitive. Most people don't
want to be jerks. But, also, most people live in their echo chambers,

hearing the voices and opinions of the people most like them. It's comfy there, but it can also be a dangerously misleading space to exist in. Criticism can seem like an attack from that vantage point. A demand for equal rights and representation can look like chaos when, in fact, it's just a balancing of the pendulum, which has always swung unfairly in one direction.

Perspective is a strange thing. It allows for the majority to, far too often, think their opinion, their "take" on something is the well-reasoned, rational, "normal," objective opinion, when it's merely the opinion that represents the experience and concerns of the majority. It doesn't necessarily make it the "wrong" opinion, but it's a mistake to automatically assume that it's the "right" opinion just because more people support it. Democracy might be a de facto popularity contest, but I can't think of a single important social movement (abolitionism, civil rights, women's rights, etc.) that ever won one of those in their early stages.

Calling Out Sexism and Rape Culture

Closer to home, a wave of anonymous online allegations of sexual misconduct—ranging from dipping one's penis in unsuspecting women's drinks to predatory rape and violence—have rocked Quebec's arts scene, forcing well-known entertainers to issue public mea culpas and bands to kick out founding members. Similar allegations about Ubisoft's toxic work culture has led to the resignation of key members of the company's upper management. Ubisoft's Montreal office has not been exempted, as many employees came forward to call out their bosses who made their working conditions a living hell. You can go ahead and call that "cancel culture" if you want, but I'm just going to go ahead and call it the consequences of s***ty behaviour.

Seriously… let's talk "cancel culture" for a minute. Who's the last person who was unjustly "cancelled" and had their ability to speak compromised or their career and life ruined? And I emphasize "unjustly" because having your career derailed, facing legal persecution or public ostracization because of legitimate accusations of sexual misconduct or racism isn't cancellation; it's just the result of your own actions.

It took upwards of 40 women to come forward for Bill Cosby to see the inside of a jail. And yet we keep worrying about these hypothetical men who've had their hypothetical lives and careers ruined. Where are they? Cancel culture has cancelled no one. Inconvenienced, maybe. Scared, for sure. Shamed, no doubt. But cancelled? I don't think so.

I may not be a fan of anonymous lists circulating, but this isn't "cancel culture." This is consequences. This is comeuppance. This is the chickens coming home to roost.

Given official statistics that point to the absurdly low number of false accusations of sexual harassment and assault, and an overwhelming majority of women (a whopping 80 per cent) who don't even report their assaults to police because they don't trust the system, shouldn't people's first impulse be to show empathy for victims? Why, instead, are they painting them as hysterical, untrustworthy, vengeful shrews engaged in a "free-for-all" takedown?

The Numbers Don't Lie and Neither Do Most Victims

There are a lot of names on that ever-growing list, but if you think that number is high you would be shocked by the number of victims whose names will never make it on there, who remain silent and always will. False allegations do happen, and they should be treated and punished with severity, but most women don't make up stories; they make up excuses about why they will never tell. Yet, instead of worrying about the alarmingly high rates of femicide, abuse, rape, violence, and crass "boys will be boys" daily disrespectful and demeaning behaviour against women, some of you seem disproportionately concerned by the extremely low possibility of false accusations against men. Why?

Sure, there's a difference between a predatory rapist and an ill-advised d*ck pic, and I would even argue that many being called out are not irredeemable villains, but average, run-of-the-mill people who've been given permission by a sexist society or celebrity idolatry to mistreat others and get away with it. But I'm also confident that none of these names have found themselves on lists out of the blue. Their past conduct (bad decision-making, crossing lines, abusing the trust and love of people around them) has, in some shape or form, placed them there. Their behaviour has been a source of trauma and now their past has caught up with them.

And once they have become part of someone's story, they don't get to decide how that person shares it. "You own everything that happened to you," says the brilliant Anne Lamott in *Bird by Bird*. "Tell your stories. If people wanted you to write warmly about them, they should have behaved better." She's talking about writing, but I can assure you she's also talking about life.

No More Tolerance for the Intolerable

We live in a world where rape and assault barely get a slap on the wrist from our justice system, where judges tell women to "keep their knees together" to keep from getting raped, where women are constantly blamed and shamed for their own assaults, so forgive me for not being particularly worried about any lasting effects for those being called out.

Most, if not all, will never face legal or any long-term social consequences. Most, if not all, will announce they're heading "into therapy" and resurface unscathed months later. Society is extremely forgiving of these "lapses of judgment" and if they are accompanied by sincere remorse and changed behaviour, they'll be easily redeemed. People can and do change, and if this wave of public denouncements forces that, we're all better for it. Those with legitimate legal cases against them might face a court of law, and what's wrong with that? Should they not face justice just because the person who likes to solicit underage kids for sex or dunk his d*ck in your Cosmo when you're not looking also happens to be someone's favourite singer?

Most victims who came forward don't even want to pursue legal action. They simply want to be heard. They want to remove this heavy weight of shame they've been carrying around and put it back where it belongs—on the abuser's shoulders. They want them to also have a sleepless night or two. They want to live in a world where behaviour like this is no longer enabled, tolerated, seen as chuckle-worthy or normal. If that's "cancel culture" I'm all in.

> *"While cancel culture is a real*
> *phenomenon that presents a clear*
> *and present danger to academic*
> *freedom, a more insidious peril*
> *lurks: the soft despotism of*
> *presumed conformity."*

Conformity Culture Is the Real Problem, Not Cancel Culture

Greg Weiner

In the following viewpoint, Greg Weiner suggests that the real problem with cancel culture is not the obvious canceling of individuals, but the culture of conformity that is created when people are afraid to speak their minds. For every individual called out for insensitive speech, Weiner asks how many never voice their opinions and are bullied into toeing the party line. Those who suppress speech often proceed from the supposition that everyone agrees with their position, which, Weiner observes, is clearly not the case. Our society has made much progress on issues such as racism, he states, but cancel culture is not aiding in this progress.

"Cancel Culture Is Not the Problem; Conformity Culture Is," by Greg Weiner, *National Review*, September 10, 2020. Reprinted by permission.

As you read, consider the following questions:

1. How does Weiner use the example of professor Jessica Krug to support his argument?
2. What does the author mean by "Maoist"?
3. What is Weiner's objection to critical race theory?

Greg Patton—a business professor, for now, at the University of Southern California, who committed the outrage of repeating a Chinese expression that sounds similar to a racist slur in English—is the latest scholar to fall prey to campus cancel culture. His case also serves as a warning that, while cancel culture is a real phenomenon that presents a clear and present danger to academic freedom, a more insidious peril lurks: the soft despotism of presumed conformity.

Patton's name is now known, and should be, to defenders of academic freedom. His case illustrates the bizarre entanglements to which cancellation is prone. He was educating students about Chinese language and culture, yet was canceled in the name of cultural diversity. Patton's lesson pertained to the use of language, yet his dean, Geoffrey Garrett, misused the obligatory word "safety" (Oxford English Dictionary: "the state of being protected from or guarded against hurt or injury") to describe the anxieties offended students felt.

All these episodes are problematic. They invert the purpose of learning, which inherently entails discomfort, as well as a baseline condition for scholarly inquiry, which is academic freedom. Patton's cancellation occupies a special, and perhaps especially absurd, category in the sense that he did not even express a controversial idea of the sort academic freedom should protect.

But there is an advantage to these explicit illustrations of cancel culture: They are visible and known. The more egregious they are, the more attention they draw. A larger question looms behind them: Who never speaks in the first place? One can imagine junior faculty, in particular, treating Patton as a cautionary tale: Offend students, get suspended. But even that is rooted in the shock and awe of prominent cases.

The more difficult cases—largely unknown because they are, unlike discrete and reportable events, unknowable—are those in which scholars restrain their own language not out of fear but rather out of weariness. For them, the question may be less what consequences will ensue from controversy than whether they have the time and energy to engage in it. Resistance is not futile; it is simply exhausting. Purported offenses and the silencing that attends them are identifiable events that tend, at least in the circles that care about them, to make news. Self-censorship, if it is even self-conscious, is the dog that never barked and is not news precisely for that reason.

The dynamic of cancellation, too, is at least tangible. People are offended. They protest audibly and demand redress. Often, their intent is reeducation and suppression. But we know when it occurs and can oppose it. To be sure, cancellation is a cudgel for conformity. Its influence as a background condition is undeniable.

But the intent of those who seek compliance more softly is not necessarily hostile or heavy-handed. They may, on the contrary, sincerely perceive themselves as charitable. The resulting dynamic is less severe and arguably more insidious: those who police, or rather shape, speech not with an intent to suppress dissent but rather on what they view to be the benevolent assumption that everyone agrees with them.

This attitude is familiar in academia and, doubtless, beyond. It is evident in conversations that are not intended to reeducate but rather to reenforce what everyone assumes everyone else already believes. Many proponents of critical race theory—whose animating idea is that race is the one thing needful, the single lens through which all other phenomena should be viewed—are indeed trying to compel compliance. But even more simply operate on the belief that everyone agrees with them. For this crowd, that is an act of sincere charity: Reasonable people agree with me, and the people I encounter are reasonable.

One suspects, for example, that the training in critical race theory that President Trump recently suspended in federal agencies is often less intended to force every individual to comply than to reflect an assumption that everyone already does. True, that gives it a bizarre cast: uniformity in the name of diversity; education centered on what is purported already to be known. But while the tone of news reporting tends to pit proponents of critical race theory against its adversaries, the most common purveyors of the softer approach to conformity may not be social-justice warriors. Warriors relish the fight. This is less war than bureaucracy. It assumes a uniformity of opinion that requires no fight, only repetitive procedures that reflect a victory already achieved. It is a mindset likelier to be puzzled than outraged by Trump's move.

That manifests in the steady deflation of language. Programs based on critical race theory, in a recent Politico headline, were matter-of-factly described as "racial equity training." Did the headline writer consciously intend to render the language benign so as to conceal the controversy that actually surrounded it? Perhaps. But, and this is the subtler and therefore more dangerous possibility, perhaps not. The casual and uncritical repetition of terms such as "systemic racism" suggests similar assumptions. Why, one might ask, are Americans signing petitions demanding individual indictments when those individual behaviors are the product of "systems"? Journalists have an interest in the integrity of words. They are a writer's raw materials. A business model that devalues them will not long sustain purveyors of those goods. A polity that traffics in contradictions will become further divided because many people will see themselves as speaking another language.

Similarly, coverage of Professor Jessica Krug—a white George Washington University professor who posed for years as African-American—paid no heed to the flagrant inversion of language in the Maoist self-denunciation ("you should absolutely cancel me; and I absolutely cancel myself") she posted on Medium.com. Krug confessed to lying. A lie (OED: "a false statement made with intent to deceive") involves the misuse of words. Yet so did the confession.

One need read no further than the headline over Krug's Medium.com post—"The Truth, and the Anti-Black Violence of My Lies"—to see that no one gave a second look to the fundamental fact that she admitted lies by deploying words as instruments of will rather than meaning. Yet on what grounds do those for whom words are fungible denounce lies? Krug's body of scholarly work was manifestly and ideologically pro-black, at least as she conceives the term. Her "lies," consisting of words, were not "violent." Among the premises of political life—Aristotle: "man is by nature a political animal"; "man alone among the animals has speech"—is that words are an explicit alternative to violence.

The inattention to some of the more shocking assertions in the post—"I don't believe that any anti-Black life has inherent value"—may reflect an assumption of consensus both as to what constitutes being "anti-Black" and the irredeemable consequences of those so characterized.

There was a similar inversion of words in a recent online town-hall meeting at Northwestern University's law school. It featured the spectacle—at once bizarre and predictable—of individuals denouncing themselves as racists and promising to "do better" in the future. Here, too, the Maoism was chilling. So was the accompanying degradation of words. The whole point of the exercise was to demonstrate that the individuals were not racist. The only way they could prove it was to declare exactly the opposite.

There is no small element of virtue signaling in all this. But the signal can be received only on a frequency on which it is presupposed to be virtuous. That notion of virtue is undermined by the inability to protest what is unjust without limitlessly extending the scope of accusation.

In that vein, it is worth noting two facts. One is that society is reckoning with issues of race right now because acts of racism are immoral and unjust. These acts should be confronted on their own terms.

Yet the premise of critical race theory is that race permeates everything. The second fact is therefore inescapable: On issues of race, the history of the United States is one of progress. The story is uneven, but the trajectory is upward. This does not mean that enough progress has been made or that acts of racism should not be confronted. But it is revealing that we are discovering that race permeates everything around us at exactly the same moment that permeation is at or near a historic low, viewed in the broad sweep of historical time. That is different from saying it is low enough. But the trajectory of allegation is almost precisely the opposite of the trajectory of progress. Among those most committed to the idea that race is everything, is it possible that race becoming less prominent is a threat?

The consensus these softer advocates of conformity assume is a twist on Tocqueville's "omnipotence of the majority." Tocqueville predicted that majority opinion would silence dissent in democracies, if only by making egalitarian individuals doubt their own opinions exactly because the multitude, composed of their equals, disagreed. Yet the assumption behind this softer and more insidious version is that no one disagrees to begin with. It is not an attempt to tyrannize through dominant opinion. It rests, rather, on an unreflective presupposition that dominant opinion is universally shared. This is not cancel culture. It is conformity culture. Each fuels the other, but the latter may prove to be a more corrosive force.

> *"Perhaps the best message as we enter
> a new year is to remain respectful
> and empathetic to others."*

Cancel Culture and Conspiracy Theories Threaten Political Legitimacy

Hugh Breakey

In the following viewpoint, Hugh Breakey argues that extremism on both the left and the right threaten what he calls "political legitimacy." Breakey defines political legitimacy as generally agreed upon laws that allow rules and public institutions to function effectively in a society. Cancel culture, which shuts down controversial voices, threatens political legitimacy in Breakey's eyes. On the political right, conspiracy theories pose a similar threat to political legitimacy. Former president Donald Trump's claim that the election was stolen from him is one such example. The solution to these dangerous trends is for those on both sides of the political spectrum to respect one another and display empathy. Hugh Breakey is president of the Australian Association for Professional & Applied Ethics.

"Conspiracy Theories on the Right, Cancel Culture on the Left: How Political Legitimacy Came Under Threat in 2020," by Hugh Breakey, The Conversation, December 31, 2020. https://theconversation.com/conspiracy-theories-on-the-right-cancel-culture-on-the-left -how-political-legitimacy-came-under-threat-in-2020-150844. Licensed under CC BY-ND 4.0 International.

As you read, consider the following questions:

1. What examples does the author offer of people who have been canceled?
2. According to the viewpoint, how have dangerous political trends manifested themselves in Australia?
3. What does the author mean when he says that ideas are "self-sealing"?

2020 has been a challenging year. For some challenges, such as the coronavirus, a light is appearing at the end of the tunnel. But for others, the true consequences may be only beginning to appear.

This is perhaps no more true than in the assault on political legitimacy. In 2020, this was threatened by forces on opposite sides of politics: cancel culture on the left and conspiracy theories on the right.

Each poses a serious threat, as a collapse in political legitimacy means people think the normal rules don't apply anymore, making the world a more difficult and even dangerous place for all of us.

What Is Political Legitimacy?

What exactly is political legitimacy and why is it important?

Let's start with a definition of legitimacy. Legitimacy, in this context, refers to whether we should accept a decision, rule or institution.

It doesn't require wholehearted agreement. For example, we might think a workplace decision is misguided, but decide that as an employee we should go along with it anyway.

Political legitimacy refers to the legitimacy of laws and authorities in the eyes of the people. It allows rules and public institutions to function effectively.

We will never all agree on exactly what the law should be—particularly in pluralistic societies. However, we can all agree that democratic decision-making is an appropriate way to make laws.

Of course, legitimacy has limits. If a democracy votes to enslave an ethnic minority, this wouldn't be acceptable. Legitimacy only works when the outcomes are tolerable.

The Perils of Cancel and Call-Out Culture

The terms "cancel culture" and "call-out culture"—which became ubiquitous in 2020, particularly on the political left—refer to practices of shutting down, shaming or deterring those who are perceived to speak in offensive or harmful ways.

Examples abound, but one notable case occurred during the Black Lives Matter protests against police brutality in the US in May.

Political analyst David Shor tweeted a summary of a Black Princeton professor's research about the historical impact of violent protests on Democratic voting. When called out for perceived anti-Blackness, Shor apologised, but was nevertheless fired.

More recently, employees at Penguin Random House in Canada lodged an official protest at the news that a sequel to Jordan Peterson's bestseller, *12 Rules for Life*, would be published. It echoed an earlier employee-led revolt against the publication of J.K. Rowling's new children's book.

Stifling and shutting down controversial voices, such as Peterson and Rowling, presents two challenges to political legitimacy.

First, it prevents inclusive dialogue. Those in the minority on any issue can no longer console themselves with the fact that at least they had the opportunity to say their piece and have their views considered. Instead, they are silenced and excluded.

Second, the idea that voters on the right have not just wrong, but harmful views poses a further threat to legitimacy.

Why should progressives respect democratic outcomes—such as the victories of Republican legislators in the 2020 US elections, or Trump's win in 2016—if these outcomes simply reflect what they perceive as the manifestly intolerable views of millions of conservative voters?

How Conspiracy Theories Undermine Democratic Legitimacy

From the opposite side of politics comes another threat: conspiracy theories.

To be sure, conspiracies do occur, but they are usually confined to close-knit groups at single organisations that excel at secrecy (for example, intelligence agencies).

Many currently popular conspiracy theories require strikingly poor reasoning practices.

Even setting aside QAnon's wacky beliefs, the idea peddled by outgoing President Donald Trump that the US election was stolen is far-fetched. No tangible evidence has been presented for this claim.

In fact, many of the institutions certifying the result were run by Republican officials, while Republican-appointed judges have thrown out many Trump campaign cases brought to court. And though Joe Biden won the presidential contest, Democrats had an unexpectedly poor showing in other races.

If Trump's claim was true, such a conspiracy would have to be far-reaching (including both Republicans and Democrats) and powerful (leaving no evidence), while at the same time being stunningly incompetent (having forgotten to ensure Democratic victories in Congress).

Yet, this theory is extraordinarily popular, with the vast majority of the president's 74 million voters believing fraud changed the election outcome.

This impacts political legitimacy because a stubborn lack of respect for evidence undermines public deliberative practices. It is impossible to find points of agreement when large-scale conspiracies throw so much into question.

Conspiracies about election results also threaten democratic legitimacy. If everything is controlled by a sinister cabal, then elections are a farce.

Worse, if one's political opponents are seen as utterly evil—for example, cannibalistic Satanic child traffickers—then not even authentic elections could legitimise their rule.

Striking Similarities

So, both conspiracy thinking and cancel culture can challenge the legitimacy of democratic decision-making.

But this is not all they have in common. Both are longstanding practices whose recent rise has been fueled by social media. Both are personally rewarding, as they allow believers to position themselves as manifestly superior to others (the "deplorables" or "sheeple").

Both views are also "self-sealing" insofar as adherents shield themselves from contrary ideas and evidence (allowing groupthink to flourish).

Cancel culture advocates never need face uncomfortable critique because opponents can simply be cancelled or called out, derailing further discussion.

And conspiracy theorists can simply dismiss critique as part of the conspiracy, or based on falsities spread by the conspiracy.

What Can Be Done?

Even in Australia, commentators have observed the woeful state of political deliberation and its impact on trust in institutions. In the wake of the Banking Royal Commission, for example, Commissioner Kenneth Haynes lamented political rhetoric now resorts to the language of war, seeking to portray opposing views as presenting existential threats to society as we now know it.

Unfortunately, because these views are self-sealing, and because they attach to people's chosen identities, there are no easy responses to them.

Still, these movements are not monolithic. Many from the left have spoken out against political intolerance, and some Republican officials in the US have stood up against Trump's conspiracy theories.

Perhaps the best message as we enter a new year is to remain respectful and empathetic to others.

At a base level, keep in mind that others may have legitimate concerns: conspiracies do happen and everyone has limits to what they will tolerate.

Rather than reacting with anger or mockery, or directly challenging someone's position, it's often best to enquire carefully into their views.

And if you disagree with them, rather than aiming to change their mind, instead try to sow a few seeds of doubt that may lead to reasonable discussion and encourage later reflection.

Periodical and Internet Sources Bibliography

The following articles have been selected to supplement the diverse views presented in this chapter.

Marianne Garvey, "From Digital Detox to Apology Tours, How Some Celebrities Come Back from Being 'Canceled,'" CNN, July 19, 2021, https://www.cnn.com/2021/07/16/entertainment/canceled -cancel-culture/index.html.

Chris Hedges, "The Contradictions of 'Cancel Culture': Where Elite Liberalism Goes to Die," Salon, February 18, 2021, https://www .salon.com/2021/02/18/the-contradictions-of-cancel-culture -where-elite-liberalism-goes-to-die/.

Afua Hirsch, "Even in Our History Month, Black People Are the Repeated Victims of Cancel Culture," *The Guardian*, October 29, 2021, https://www.theguardian.com/commentisfree/2021/oct/29 /even-in-our-history-month-black-people-are-the-repeated -victims-of-cancel-culture.

Danielle Kurtzleben, "When Republicans Attack 'Cancel Culture,' What Does It Mean?" NPR, February 10, 2021, https://www.npr .org/2021/02/10/965815679/is-cancel-culture-the-future-of-the -gop.

Ryan Lizza. "Americans Tune In to 'Cancel Culture'—and Don't Like What They See," Politico, July 22, 2020, https://www.politico.com /news/2020/07/22/americans-cancel-culture-377412.

Ligaya Mishan, "The Long and Tortured History of Cancel Culture," *New York Times*, December 3, 2020, https://www.nytimes .com/2020/12/03/t-magazine/cancel-culture-history.html.

Kliph Nesteroff, "Op-Ed: 'Cancel Culture' Has Always Been a Problem for Comedy," *Los Angeles Times*, October 15, 2021, https://www.latimes.com/opinion/story/2021-10-15/cancel -culture-comedy-history-chappelle.

Evan Nierman, "Be Careful: Cancel Culture Is Here to Stay," *Forbes*, October 5, 2021, https://www.forbes.com/sites /theyec/2021/10/05/be-careful-cancel-culture-is-here-to-stay/.

Dino Sossi, "Can We Cancel 'Cancel Culture'?" The Conversation, July 21, 2021, https://theconversation.com/can-we-cancel -cancel-culture-164666.

CHAPTER 2

Is Opposition to the 1619 Project and Critical Race Theory Censorship?

Chapter Preface

Fox News, as is its bent, has America all worked up over something most citizens had not even heard of before the network began its blitz. Its talking heads are all agog over the chance to discuss critical race theory (CRT), and to a lesser extent, the 1619 Project. Both CRT and the 1619 Project are designed to cast a critical eye on race in America, its history, and its inequities. Liberals contend that these studies are a chance to correct centuries of racial injustice. Conservatives, schooled by right wing media, believe that continuing the discussion of race is only dividing America further.

Most people still don't know what CRT and 1619 really are. An anecdote that went viral on the internet offers insight into this confusion. A teacher at a private school was asked by a concerned parent whether she was teaching CRT. The teacher suggested that the parent tell her what CRT was and that, then, the teacher could tell the parent if she was teaching it. The parent was unable to answer.

Critical race theory is an academic study, until now mostly confined to law schools and graduate programs, that looks at how inequities are ingrained and codified in American systems: in the law, in business, and in society. From this starting point, CRT becomes much more intricate and complex. Because of this, its opponents have found it easy to misrepresent and attack it.

The 1619 Project, which is entirely separate from CRT, is a journalistic effort, begun by the *New York Times*, that, according to the *New York Times Magazine*'s Jake Silverstein, "aims to reframe the country's history by placing the consequences of slavery and the contributions of Black Americans at the very center of the United States' national narrative." The date, 1619, refers to the arrival of the first enslaved Africans to the Virginia colony.

Before all of the flapdoodle hit the mainstream right wing media, few teachers in America had heard of CRT, much less taught it in classrooms. As recently as May 2021, *Education Week*, which bills itself as "the #1 source of high-quality news and insights on K-12 education," published what amounts to a primer on CRT, entitled, "What Is Critical Race Theory, and Why Is It Under Attack?" Now, with students beginning to ask what the outcry is all about, many teachers have no choice but to at least answer their students' questions. It seems as if Fox and its ilk have engineered a manufactured crisis: They warned about teachers bringing up CRT and 1619. Now, the teachers almost have to do so in order to remain effective. As one teacher, Jania Hoover, wrote in Vox, "The reality is that kids are talking about race, systems of oppression, and our country's ugly past anyway—from media coverage to last summer's protests to even this very controversy itself, my students are absorbing these conversations and want to know more."

Conservative parents are now showing up at school board meetings across America, demanding to know if their children are being indoctrinated. Some have argued, as did one Michigan parent, that CRT is teaching his daughter that her mother, a white woman, is evil, and is influencing children of different races to hate each other, according to a *Newsweek* article by Emma Mayer.

Republicans have begun to use white fear of CRT as a wedge issue. Virginia Republican gubernatorial candidate Glenn Youngkin made CRT a centerpiece of his ultimately victorious campaign. "We're going to embrace our parents, not ignore them," he told his overwhelmingly white crowds. "We're going to press forward with a curriculum that includes listening to parents."

If Republicans continue to see favorable election results, CRT is likely to be a prominent issue going forward.

> "Critical race theory is the newest
> manufactured wedge issue, and it's
> following a pattern we've seen with
> others recently. A cultural squall pops
> up, gets amplified on cable news and
> turns into a political storm."

Why Republicans Oppose
Critical Race Theory

Barbara Sprunt

In the following viewpoint, a transcript of a National Public Radio (NPR) report, Barbara Sprunt discusses critical race theory, a highly complex, academic theory that essentially holds that racism is embedded in American institutions. Republicans have used CRT as a culture wars wedge issue. They assert that CRT is designed to divide American society and make white people feel bad. This simplification of CRT is promoted by media outlets such as Fox News and is seen by many as an issue that may influence future elections in favor of Republicans. Barbara Sprunt is a producer on NPR's Washington desk, where she reports and produces breaking news and feature political content.

As you read, consider the following questions:

1. Why are parents showing up at school board meetings to protest CRT?
2. What is conservative activist Christopher Rufo's role in demonizing CRT?
3. How did former president Donald Trump act to curtail discussions of topics related to race?

L ULU GARCIA-NAVARRO, HOST:

It may be time for summer break. Schools are closing, but there's a lot of agita still about textbooks and lesson plans. Here's some tape from Fox News.

(SOUNDBITE OF FOX NEWS MONTAGE)

UNIDENTIFIED PERSON #1: Critical race theory is racist.

UNIDENTIFIED PERSON #2: These theories that are not based in fact.

UNIDENTIFIED PERSON #3: CRT is racist. It is abusive.

GARCIA-NAVARRO: Critical race theory is the newest manufactured wedge issue, and it's following a pattern we've seen with others recently. A cultural squall pops up, gets amplified on cable news and turns into a political storm. NPR's Barbara Sprunt is going to take us through how an obscure academic theory now has parents laying siege to school board meetings. And she joins us now. Hi, Barbara.

BARBARA SPRUNT, BYLINE: Good morning.

GARCIA-NAVARRO: We need to start with what critical race theory is and what it is not.

SPRUNT: Because they are very different things. In the late '70s, early '80s, legal scholars developed an academic approach that examines American institutions and laws through the lens of race and racism. So it's been around for decades, and it's used in postgraduate studies. But many Republicans and right-wing media have co-opted this term, and they're using it as a catch-all way of describing basically any conversation about race or racism that makes white people uncomfortable. So conversations about white privilege, having dialogues about anti-racism—these have all been branded falsely as critical race theory.

GARCIA-NAVARRO: In September of 2020, President Trump issued the executive order on combating race and sex stereotyping, which President Biden has rescinded. Trump's EO didn't actually mention critical race theory then, even in the sections specifying what shouldn't be taught in the armed forces or at federal agencies. It has been mentioned a lot on Fox, though.

(SOUNDBITE OF FOX NEWS BROADCAST)

CHRISTOPHER RUFO: It's absolutely astonishing how critical race theory has pervaded every institution in the federal government. And what I've discovered is that critical race theory has become, in essence, the default ideology of the federal bureaucracy and is now being weaponized against the American people.

GARCIA-NAVARRO: Now, that's Christopher Rufo on September 2, 2020. Talk to us about his role in all this.

SPRUNT: Yeah. So Rufo is a central player in this. He's a former documentarian, and he's the one who called on Trump to issue that executive order you just mentioned. And this all started in July of 2020. A Seattle city employee sent Rufo an antibias training that they did at work, and Rufo essentially saw it as a political opportunity to manufacture a culture war issue. And he's been transparent about that. I mean, he tweeted in March of this year that, quote, "the goal is to have the public read something crazy in the newspaper and immediately think critical race theory."

And he added that he's rebranding the theory and driving up negative perceptions to turn it toxic. And, I mean, it's worked. I mean, you can go on Twitter and type in critical race theory, and you'll see videos of hundreds of parents at school board meetings with signs saying, stop critical race theory, even as the superintendents are saying, hey, this is not something that we teach. Saying critical race theory is being taught in schools is like saying electrical engineering is being taught in K-12. It's just not happening.

GARCIA-NAVARRO: But when you talk to conservative lawmakers, what are they saying?

SPRUNT: Well, the overall argument is that talking about race and racism leads to more division in an already very divided country. Byron Donalds is a Republican congressman from Florida, and he told me recently that, look. It's important to teach the full history of the country, but he thinks that the approach just further divides Americans.

BYRON DONALDS: As a Black man, I think our history has actually been quite awful. I mean, that's without question. But you also have to take into account the progression of our country, especially over the last 60 to 70 years.

SPRUNT: You'll also hear some Republican lawmakers and media outlets say, you know, this theory is unpatriotic. It tells white people that they're racist, you know, just for being white, when, of course, the actual theory itself is about institutions, not individuals.

GARCIA-NAVARRO: Right. It's about the systems that are in play and how that has actually created more difficulties for Black and brown people. But there is an actual legislative movement on this.

It's not just people talking about critical race theory. They're actually legislating about it now, right?

SPRUNT: That's right. I mean, this is something where perception has led to actual movement in legislatures. Republican lawmakers in nearly two dozen states have proposed legislation that would limit how teachers can talk about race and racism in the classroom. Now, just like you pointed out earlier, that Trump's executive order on this didn't actually mention critical race theory, that's the same thing that you're seeing here on the state level. Only a handful of these bills explicitly mention critical race theory, but they're moving forward regardless.

GARCIA-NAVARRO: As we've discussed, critical race theory is a technical term. It's sort of a framework for graduate programs. So money isn't being spent on it in public grade schools, you know, teaching it to young people. But that doesn't seem to stop people getting upset.

SPRUNT: Exactly. I mean, this is a perfect culture war issue. Unlike issues like taxes or foreign policy, this is something that strikes people at their very identity. And that's what makes it an effective political strategy, to be honest. I spoke with Christine Matthews. She's the president of Bellwether Research and a public opinion pollster, and she says there's evidence that Republican voters have been responding much more to culture issues and that this issue could impact turnout in next year's midterm elections.

CHRISTINE MATTHEWS: I think it's just one more addition to the culture war that the Republicans really want to fight. And Republicans are wanting to make this about othering the Democrats and making them seem as extreme and threatening to white culture as possible.

GARCIA-NAVARRO: And I guess that brings us right back to the right-wing media ecosystem because it's easier to conflate anything related to race with critical race theory, especially if you don't understand what it is.

SPRUNT: Exactly. And from a messaging perspective, critical race theory is easy to use and is being used as an umbrella term to cover all sorts of white grievances about how society is talking about anti-racism, you know, particularly in the year following the murder of George Floyd. And Matthews says that talk news can really keep this issue top of mind for voters, even though the midterms are over a year away.

MATTHEWS: That's the job of Fox News—is to keep these cultural, polarizing topics front of mind. And so for the base and for the people that, say, Fox News reaches, they can keep it alive if they want to.

SPRUNT: And it seems like they want to. A study from Media Matters, a left-leaning nonprofit, recently found that nearly 1,300 mentions of critical race theory were on Fox News over a 3 1/2-month period.

GARCIA-NAVARRO: Wow.

SPRUNT: Another, you know, important factor in this is the role of social media. Experts I spoke with said this is just another prime example of something that gets posted on Facebook and just takes on a life of its own. And if that's where people are getting their information, their news, they're going to be getting a lot of misinformation.

GARCIA-NAVARRO: That's NPR's Barbara Sprunt. Thank you very much.

SPRUNT: Thank you.

> *"Research points to the benefits of high-quality discussion of controversial issues, such as growth in tolerance for other points of view, interest in politics and knowledge about the issues students investigate."*

Students Benefit from Tackling Controversial Issues

Judith Pace

In the following viewpoint, Judith Pace argues that when children live through traumatic times, they often bring their anxieties and concerns to the classroom. In these turbulent political times, children can benefit from discussions of controversial topics in the classroom. Discussion of multicultural issues should be a focus in classrooms. Yet, Pace asserts, such conversations rarely take place. Educational leaders should promote such learning and prepare teachers to tackle difficult subjects in the classroom. Judith L. Pace is a professor of teacher education at the University of San Francisco and author of The Charged Classroom: Predicaments and Possibilities for Democratic Teaching.

As you read, consider the following questions:

1. Why do sustained discussions of controversial topics rarely occur in the classroom?
2. Which students often have fewer opportunities for fruitful discussions in the classroom?
3. What are some resources the author suggests for preparing educators to tackle controversial topics?

As a series of seemingly never-ending horrific events dominates news headlines, children are especially vulnerable to the fear and anxiety these attacks can provoke.

More than ever, young people are exposed to violent and traumatic confrontations at home and abroad through social media. They feel the ripple effects of these and other disturbing events, which may threaten their own and their loved ones' sense of well-being.

Inevitably, children bring these incidents, and their reactions to them, to school. Even the vitriolic rhetoric of the presidential campaign is having an impact on children. For example, a non-representative online survey of 2,000 teachers, titled "The Trump Effect: The Impact of the Presidential Campaign on Our Nation's Schools," was conducted by the Southern Poverty Law Center. It concluded that the campaign is "producing an alarming level of fear and anxiety among children of color, and inflaming racial and ethnic tensions in the classroom."

It would make sense for educators to prepare this summer for the reverberations of these intensely charged events inside classrooms and schools. This preparation should involve four vital elements: 1) understanding how they affect children of different ages, identities and communities; 2) learning how to facilitate constructive dialogue among students about current issues; 3) making learning about the democratic process a priority for all students; and 4) helping teachers grapple with increased tensions in society that play out in their work with students.

We know that classroom life is shaped by external forces in schools and society. For example, ongoing tensions among different racial, socioeconomic and religious groups that play out in schools will likely be heightened by what feels like a chaotic sociopolitical climate. At the same time, this year's events, including the presidential election, provide possibilities for engaging students in what educators call "democratic learning" in the context of a multicultural society.

In addition to formal instruction in civics, democratic learning involves developing dispositions and skills to engage in democratic practices through active involvement in them. These practices include discussing controversial issues and making informed group decisions. Multicultural democratic learning includes developing appreciation for human diversity, the experiences of historically marginalized groups, and their struggles for equal rights. An example of a multicultural democratic learning opportunity is discussion of inter-group conflict from multiple points of view, which can produce critical thinking, deeper understanding of complex problems, and the ability to participate in civil discourse across differences.

Research points to the benefits of high-quality discussion of controversial issues, such as growth in tolerance for other points of view, interest in politics and knowledge about the issues students investigate. But researchers also find that sustained discussion of controversy rarely occurs in classrooms. This is due to concerns such as losing control of their classroom, retribution from administrators and community members, a lack of the skills needed to effectively teach these controversial issues, and competing demands such as the pressure to focus on academic outcomes and make sure students score well on standardized tests.

Demographic diversity among students also contributes to avoidance of taking on controversy in the classroom due to fear of conflict.

In fact, students of color, students at low-income schools and those in low-track classes have significantly fewer opportunities to learn about democratic processes than do their white, higher-income, college-bound peers. Equalizing democratic learning opportunities, which lead to increased political engagement and knowledge, should be a priority.

These volatile times call for helping teachers learn how to promote constructive discussions of charged issues with all their classes. Whether planned or not, these issues will get raised, if not by teachers, then by their students. We can be sure that young people, like adults, will feel compelled to discuss them to try and make sense of them. Classroom teachers and the professionals who support them—school leaders, teacher educators and professional developers—need to prepare for and take educational advantage of the disequilibrium created by these events. In fact, teacher educators and school administrators should lead the way by modeling constructive talk about difficult topics in their own practice.

Resources for facilitating discussion of difficult and controversial issues are plentiful. For those interested in research, Diana Hess's book *Controversy in the Classroom* and *The Political Classroom*, by Hess and Paula McAvoy, are excellent resources. The Southern Poverty Law Center's Teaching Tolerance website offers Teaching about Race, Racism, and Police Violence as well as many other tools. Facing History and Ourselves also provides materials on a wide range of topics. Valerie Strauss of the *Washington Post* published a list of resources in her column. University websites have posted guidelines for discussion, especially in the wake of campus protests.

Promoting constructive dialogue about controversy is a matter of educational will. It involves risks for teachers. To give them adequate support, school leaders, communities and policy makers must get behind multicultural democratic education as a central purpose of schooling. Learning to do it well takes time. Now is the time to start.

> *"Despite mainstream media and educators' claims that teachers are not applying CRT, examples to the contrary abound."*

Critical Race Theory Has Infiltrated Math and Science

Jonathan Butcher

In the following viewpoint, Jonathan Butcher argues that critical race theory (CRT) is a "toxic narrative" that is inherently racist, and that it is not only being promoted in schools but is even being taught in classes that he believes have nothing to do with race, such as math and science. The author states that legislation such as the Civil Rights Act (1964) and the emergence of state and federal agencies designed to stop and prosecute racist acts have done enough to end racism in the United States and that further discussions of racism are unproductive, divisive, and racist. Jonathan Butcher is the Will Skillman Fellow in Education at the Heritage Foundation. He is the author of Splintered: Critical Race Theory and the Progressive War on Truth.

"Rescuing Math and Science from Critical Race Theory's Racial Discrimination," by Jonathan Butcher, The Heritage Foundation, July 13, 2021. Reprinted by permission.

As you read, consider the following questions:

1. According to the author, what is toxic about critical race theory?
2. What are some examples of critical race theory being taught in public school classes?
3. What evidence does Butcher supply to support his claim that CRT is "overt racial discrimination"?

P roponents of critical race theory are not just indoctrinating students with their toxic narrative in history classes, but even in math and science.

Educators around the country are applying critical race theory (CRT) to K–12 lesson plans. CRT is a worldview that makes racial identity the prism through which its advocates consider all aspects of public and private life. Critical race theorists believe that racial discrimination against the "oppressors" is not only appropriate, but necessary, and that public and private institutions—government and businesses, for example—must generate equal outcomes for everyone.[1] Despite mainstream media and educators' claims that teachers are not applying CRT,[2] examples to the contrary abound:

- In Portland, Oregon, the Portland Public School District hosted a "Critical Race Theory Coalition Summit" this past April.[3]
- The Loudon County Public School District contracted with an organization called The Equity Collaborative to provide professional development to district teachers. The Equity Collaborative prioritizes CRT in its training.[4]
- The California Department of Education created a model ethnic-studies curriculum that is replete with CRT's racially discriminatory ideas, including "intersectionality."[5] Kimberlé Crenshaw, one of CRT's originators, designed this concept, which claims that all ethnic minorities are oppressed in American society and that they are oppressed in multiple

ways—based on their gender, class, race, and other combinations of racial and personal characteristics.[6]

Since CRT is a philosophy or worldview (fields of study that are considered "soft" sciences), educators have applied the theory to other soft sciences (or non-hard sciences), such as history and civics.[7] Educators who have adopted CRT's perspective on these subjects accuse America's public and private institutions (government and businesses, for example) as being "systemically racist," arguing that the effects of slavery and the Jim Crow era persist today. Early CRT thinkers, such as Derrick Bell, stated this position in their writings.[8]

Critical race theorists who are active in K–12 education today have created lessons in history, civics, and social studies that incorporate CRT and its concepts of systemic racism and intersectionality. For example, the Zinn Education Project, which continues the work of revisionist historian Howard Zinn, provides lessons that teach that "structural racism" remains present in America, despite the Civil Rights Act's prohibitions against racial discrimination.[9]

Some social studies lessons, such as one entitled "The Color Line," state directly that the lesson is part of a "quest to construct [a] critical perspective."[10] The word "critical" here does not refer to desirable critical thinking, but to CRT. The Black Lives Matter at School recommended that curricular materials include lessons on how to apply CRT, with school systems using the materials to teach that America is systemically racist.[11]

Critical Race Theory and K–12 Math and Science Curricula

Educators are also applying CRT's racial bias to math and science. Colleges of education—where teachers are trained before entering the classroom—have produced materials that teach educators how to use CRT in these subjects for many years. In 2014, the Columbia Teachers College Record released a report titled "When It Comes to Mathematics Experiences of Black Pre-Service Teachers...Race

Matters," in which the author says that, according to critical race theorists, even math has an "identity."[12]

Consistent with other critical race theorists, such as Richard Delgado, Jean Stefancic, and Ibram X. Kendi, the author rejects colorblindness and makes accusations of ongoing privileges based on white skin color:

> CRT has been used along with other race-centered frameworks in mathematics education to expose the practices of some White mathematics teachers who profess racial indifference and colorblindness, while dismissing discussions of White privilege and antiracist pedagogy.[13]

In February 2021, the National Council of Teachers of Mathematics (NCTM) recommended *Critical Race Theory in Mathematics Education* to its members for summer reading.[14] NCTM's keynote speaker at its 2019 conference was the critical race theorist and college professor Gloria Ladson-Billings. (One of Ladson-Billings's most-cited articles is titled, "Just What Is Critical Race Theory and What's It Doing in a Nice Field Like Education?"[15])

Likewise, the National Science Teaching Association wrote in May 2020 that its members now "work from the stance that scientific ways of knowing and science education are fundamentally cultural and inherently political."[16] The organization recently hosted a multi-day online event that included a session titled "Critical Affinity Spaces for Science Educators," where teachers were taught to use a "critical lens that…exposes the hidden and master narratives" in science, and affirms "that racial/social justice approaches to science teaching are needed." Just as with the 2019 NCTM conference, the organization featured a proponent of CRT as the keynote speaker.[17]

Predictably, then, school officials who are either sympathetic to, or unaware of, CRT's discriminatory ideas are following these organizations and designing K–12 math and science curricula using CRT's false and dangerous precepts:

- District officials from Los Angeles, San Diego, and other California school districts created "Equitable Math."

This math curriculum opens with recommendations for "critical approaches to dismantling white supremacy in math classrooms" and encourages "critical praxis" (the use of CRT in teaching practices).[18] "White supremacy" is mentioned 54 times in the curriculum's first handbook, with no mention of addition, subtraction, or any other skills. Portland Public Schools, home to the Critical Race Theory Coalition mentioned above, is using the curriculum.[19] The California Department of Education recently updated its math standards, recommending that teachers ask students completing mathematical word problems to ask questions such as "Who [sic] does this privilege? Who [sic] does this silence?"[20]

- In 2019, Seattle Public Schools created a "K–12 Math Ethnic Studies Framework" that divided math instruction into the CRT themes of "Origins, Identity, and Agency"; "Power and Oppression"; "History of Resistance and Liberation"; and "Reflection and Action"—terms identical to or consistent with the teacher training materials referenced above. (Seattle school officials did not mandate that local schools use the framework, though the material is still available on the district's website.)[21]

- Groups such as Learning for Justice, an arm of the extreme leftist Southern Poverty Law Center, recommends science lessons on the "social construction of race" and to consider "why science looks the way it does," that is, why more ethnic minorities are not active in scientific research.[22]

- In Boston, teachers told the *Boston Globe* last fall that they will "teach about…naming conventions in scientific laws and theorems rooted in European colonization."[23] The teacher said, "We're naming things [in science] because of colonial influence, because of imperialism." On average, black fourth-grade students score 33 points below their white peers on a national comparison in science. Educators should spend more time focusing on scientific facts rather than addressing and manufacturing political content unrelated to basic science.

Policy Recommendations

With district and state educators revising instruction in math and the hard sciences away from facts and skills, parents, teachers, and policymakers should:

- Request copies of public school instructional materials, reject content that teaches racial discrimination, and consider proposals that prohibit the use of content that violates Title VI of the Civil Rights Act of 1964; and
- Design proposals that offer education savings accounts, as available in Arizona, Florida, and North Carolina, to name a few states, to students attending schools teaching racially discriminatory content.[24]

Policymakers should:

- Revoke the state K–12 funding for public schools that teach or apply racial discrimination in any subjects.

Conclusion

Critical race theory is overt racial discrimination. Theorists claim that America is systemically racist, despite the Civil Rights Act and state and federal agencies designed to stop and prosecute racist acts. And despite the enormous and obvious progress on race that this country has made.

Educators have used CRT to redesign history, civics, and English instructional content to focus on the critical obsession with oppression and power. Now, school officials are also changing classroom content in the hard sciences and math away from facts and skills and focusing on racial activism. (In math!) Parents, teachers, and policymakers should oppose any form of racial discrimination in schools, and reject these insidious efforts to inject prejudice and racial bias into technical subjects that should be used to help children—of all backgrounds—to develop skills and abilities that will help them to be successful in school and in life.

Notes

1. See, for example, Ibram X. Kendi, How to Be an Antiracist (New York: One World, 2019), pp. 18 and 19, and Richard Delgado and Jean Stefancic, eds., Critical Race Theory: An Introduction (New York: New York University Press, 2001), pp. 7 and 8.
2. John Battiston, "Ziegler Remains Firm LCPS Is 'Not Teaching Critical Race Theory,'" Loudon Times-Mirror, June 3, 2021, https://www.loudountimes.com/news /ziegler-remains-firm-lcps-is-not-teaching-critical-race-theory/article_146c1e8c -c3c9-11eb-9217-ebb5be4d3868.html (accessed July 7, 2021); "Explained: The Truth about Critical Race Theory and How It Shows Up in Your Child's Classroom," Education Post, May 5, 2021, https://educationpost.org/explained -the-truth-about-critical-race-theory-and-how-it-shows-up-in-your-childs- classroom/ (accessed July 9, 2021); and Kiara Alfonseca, "Critical Race Theory in the Classroom: Understanding the Debate," ABC News, May 19, 2021, https:// abcnews.go.com/US/critical-race-theory-classroom-understanding-debate /story?id=77627465 (accessed July 7, 2021).
3. PPS Communications, "Portland Public Schools Critical Race Theory CRiT Coalition Summit," April 22, 2021, video, YouTube.com, https://www.youtube.com /watch?v=tt980kX5KMI&t=3773s (accessed July 7, 2021).
4. Equity Collaborative, "Introduction to Critical Race Theory," On-Line Institute, May 7, 2020, https://theequitycollaborative.com/wp-content/uploads/2020/05/Intro -To-Critical-Race-Theory.pdf (accessed July 7, 2021); news release, "How Critical Race Theory Infected Loudon County Public Schools," Fight for Schools, May 26, 2021, https://fightforschools.com/news/f/how-critical-race-theory-infected -loudoun-county-public-schools (accessed July 7, 2021); and "Loudon County Public Schools Service Agreement" with The Equity Collaborative, https:// documentcloud.adobe.com/link/track?uri=urn:aaid:scds:US:ae15f1d7-d4be-4153 -9014-aef334b3c1b6#pageNum=1 (accessed July 7, 2021).
5. California Department of Education, "Ethnic Studies Model Curriculum," Chapters 1 and 4, https://www.cde.ca.gov/ci/cr/cf/esmc.aspl (accessed July 9, 2021).
6. Kimberlé Crenshaw, "Demarginalizing the Intersection of Race and Sex: A Black Feminist Critique of Antidiscrimination Doctrine, Feminist Theory and Antiracist Politics," University of Chicago Legal Forum, Vol. 1989, No. 1, Article 8 (1989), https://chicagounbound.uchicago.edu/cgi/viewcontent.cgi ?article=1052&context=uclf (accessed July 7, 2021).
7. See, for example, LaGarrett J. King, "Black History Is Not American History: Toward a Framework of Black Historical Consciousness," Social Education, Vol. 84, No. 6 (November/December 2020), pp. 335–341, https://www.socialstudies.org/sites /default/files/view-article-2020-12/se8406335.pdf (accessed July 7, 2021).
8. Derrick Bell, "David C. Baum Memorial Lecture: Who's Afraid of Critical Race Theory?" University of Illinois Law Review, Vol. 1995, No. 4 (February 1995), pp. 900 and 901.
9. Zinn Education Project, "Clint Smith on Teaching about Structural Racism," June 12, 2019, https://www.zinnedproject.org/news/clint-smith-teach-structural-racism/ (accessed July 7, 2021).
10. Zinn Education Project, "The Color Line," https://www.zinnedproject.org/materials /color-line-colonial-laws (accessed July 7, 2021).
11. D.C. Area Educators for Social Justice, "D.C. Area Black Lives Matter Week of Action," https://www.dcareaeducators4socialjustice.org/black-lives-matter/resources (accessed July 7, 2021), and Black Lives Matter at School, "BLM@School/

Disability Justice Resources Sampler! (Resources)," "Using Critical Race Theory," https://padlet.com/christopher_r_r/b0yr3nsfquhudpt9 (accessed July 7, 2021).

12. Ebony O. McGee, "When It Comes to Mathematics Experiences of Black Pre-Service Teachers…Race Matters," Teachers College Record, Vol. 116, No. 6 (2014).

13. Ibid.; Kendi, How to Be an Antiracist, p. 9; and Delgado and Stefancic, Critical Race Theory: An Introduction, p. 12.

14. National Council of Teachers of Mathematics, "What to Read? My Summer Reading List," February 16, 2021, https://www.nctm.org/Search/?query=critical%20 race%20theory#?wst=8d68e8aabd224087f95eead8b1570035 (accessed July 7, 2021).

15. National Council of Teachers of Mathematics, "2019 NCTM San Diego Annual Conference Program & Presentation," https://www.nctm.org/Conferences-and-Professional-Development/Annual-Meeting-and-Exposition/Program-and-Presentation/ (accessed July 7, 2021), and National Academy of Education, "Gloria Ladson-Billings," https://naeducation.org/our-members/gloria-ladson-billings/ (accessed July 9, 2021).

16. National Science Teaching Association, "Social Justice in the Science Classroom," May 26, 2020, https://www.nsta.org/blog/social-justice-science-classroom (accessed July 7, 2021).

17. National Science Teaching Association, "Virtual Miniseries: What IS Social Justice Teaching in the Science Classroom?" https://www.nsta.org/social-justice-series-2 (accessed July 7, 2021).

18. Equitable Math, "Stride 1: A Pathway to Equitable Math Instruction," pp. 1, 3, and 10, https://equitablemath.org/wp-content/uploads/sites/2/2020/11/1_STRIDE1.pdf (accessed July 7, 2021).

19. Lincoln Graves, "Debate Emerges Over Racism and White Supremacy in Oregon Math Instruction," KATU ABC Channel 2, February 26, 2021, https://katu.com/news /local/debate-emerges-over-racism-and-white-supremacy-in-math-instruction (accessed July 7, 2021).

20. California Department of Education, "Mathematics Framework: 2021 Revision of the Mathematics Framework," Chapter 2: Teaching for Equity and Engagement, p. 44, https://www.cde.ca.gov/ci/ma/cf/ (accessed July 7, 2021).

21. Seattle Public Schools, "K–12 Math Ethnic Studies Framework," August 20, 2019, https://www.k12.wa.us/sites/default/files/public/socialstudies/pubdocs/Math%20 SDS%20ES%20Framework.pdf (accessed July 7, 2021), and Catherine Gewertz, "Teaching Math Through a Social Justice Lens," Education Week, December 2, 2020, https://www.edweek.org/teaching-learning/teaching-math-through-a-social-justice-lens/2020/12 (accessed July 7, 2021).

22. Shinae Park and Moses Rifkin, "Use the Tools of Science to Recognize Inequity in Science," Teaching Tolerance, April 14, 2021, https://www.learningforjustice.org /magazine/use-the-tools-of-science-to-recognize-inequity-in-science (accessed July 7, 2021).

23. Deanna Pan, "How Teachers Are Bringing Lessons from the Racial Justice Uprisings into the Classroom," The Boston Globe, September 18, 2020, https://www .bostonglobe.com/2020/09/18/metro/how-teachers-are-bringing-lessons-racial -justice-uprisings-into-classroom/ (accessed July 7, 2021).

24. Ed Choice, "Education Savings Accounts (ESAs)," https://www.edchoice.org/school -choice/types-of-school-choice/education-savings-account/ (accessed July 7, 2021).

> *"Critical race theory is a field of intellectual inquiry that demonstrates the legal codification of racism in America."*

Racial Problems Don't Go Away by Ignoring Them

David Miguel Gray

In the following viewpoint, David Miguel Gray suggests that in order to understand critical race theory (CRT), one must first understand the history of African American rights in the United States. Despite a number of legal victories, no practical progress was made to narrow the wealth gap between Blacks and whites. Critical race theory is a field of intellectual inquiry that examines why this gap persists and how racism is codified in the American legal system. Critical race theory does not demonize white people, Gray asserts. What it does do is acknowledge that racism does not simply disappear when it is ignored. David Miguel Gray is assistant professor of philosophy at the University of Memphis's Institute for Intelligent Systems.

As you read, consider the following questions:

1. What "Black Codes" were legalized in the aftermath of the Civil War?
2. What are the common beliefs among proponents of critical race theory?
3. According to the viewpoint, how is critical race theory misrepresented by its detractors?

U.S. Rep. Jim Banks of Indiana sent a letter to fellow Republicans on June 24, 2021, stating: "As Republicans, we reject the racial essentialism that critical race theory teaches ... that our institutions are racist and need to be destroyed from the ground up."

Kimberlé Crenshaw, a law professor and central figure in the development of critical race theory, said in a recent interview that critical race theory "just says, let's pay attention to what has happened in this country, and how what has happened in this country is continuing to create differential outcomes. ... Critical Race Theory ... is more patriotic than those who are opposed to it because ... we believe in the promises of equality. And we know we can't get there if we can't confront and talk honestly about inequality."

Rep. Banks' account is demonstrably false and typical of many people publicly declaring their opposition to critical race theory. Crenshaw's characterization, while true, does not detail its main features. So what is critical race theory and what brought it into existence?

The development of critical race theory by legal scholars such as Derrick Bell and Crenshaw was largely a response to the slow legal progress and setbacks faced by African Americans from the end of the Civil War, in 1865, through the end of the civil rights era, in 1968. To understand critical race theory, you need to first understand the history of African American rights in the U.S.

The History

After 304 years of enslavement, then-former slaves gained equal protection under the law with passage of the 14th Amendment in 1868. The 15th Amendment, in 1870, guaranteed voting rights for men regardless of race or "previous condition of servitude."

Between 1866 and 1877—the period historians call "Radical Reconstruction"—African Americans began businesses, became involved in local governance and law enforcement and were elected to Congress.

This early progress was subsequently diminished by state laws throughout the American South called "Black Codes," which limited voting rights, property rights and compensation for work; made it illegal to be unemployed or not have documented proof of employment; and could subject prisoners to work without pay on behalf of the state. These legal rollbacks were worsened by the spread of "Jim Crow" laws throughout the country requiring segregation in almost all aspects of life.

Grassroots struggles for civil rights were constant in post-Civil War America. Some historians even refer to the period from the New Deal Era, which began in 1933, to the present as "The Long Civil Rights Movement."

The period stretching from *Brown v. Board of Education* in 1954, which found school segregation to be unconstitutional, to the Fair Housing Act of 1968, which prohibited discrimination in housing, was especially productive.

The civil rights movement used practices such as civil disobedience, nonviolent protest, grassroots organizing and legal challenges to advance civil rights. The U.S.'s need to improve its image abroad during the Cold War importantly aided these advancements. The movement succeeded in banning explicit legal discrimination and segregation, promoted equal access to work and housing and extended federal protection of voting rights.

However, the movement that produced legal advances had no effect on the increasing racial wealth gap between Blacks and whites, while school and housing segregation persisted.

What Critical Race Theory Is

Critical race theory is a field of intellectual inquiry that demonstrates the legal codification of racism in America.

Through the study of law and U.S. history, it attempts to reveal how racial oppression shaped the legal fabric of the U.S. Critical race theory is traditionally less concerned with how racism manifests itself in interactions with individuals and more concerned with how racism has been, and is, codified into the law.

There are a few beliefs commonly held by most critical race theorists.

First, race is not fundamentally or essentially a matter of biology, but rather a social construct. While physical features and geographic origin play a part in making up what we think of as race, societies will often make up the rest of what we think of as race. For instance, 19th- and early-20th-century scientists and politicians frequently described people of color as intellectually or morally inferior, and used those false descriptions to justify oppression and discrimination.

Second, these racial views have been codified into the nation's foundational documents and legal system. For evidence of that, look no further than the "Three-Fifths Compromise" in the Constitution, whereby slaves, denied the right to vote, were nonetheless treated as part of the population for increasing congressional representation of slave-holding states.

Third, given the pervasiveness of racism in our legal system and institutions, racism is not aberrant, but a normal part of life.

Fourth, multiple elements, such as race and gender, can lead to kinds of compounded discrimination that lack the civil rights protections given to individual, protected categories. For example, Crenshaw has forcibly argued that there is a lack of legal protection for Black women as a category. The courts have treated Black women as Black, or women, but not both in discrimination cases— despite the fact that they may have experienced discrimination because they were both.

These beliefs are shared by scholars in a variety of fields who explore the role of racism in areas such as education, health care and history.

Finally, critical race theorists are interested not just in studying the law and systems of racism, but in changing them for the better.

What Critical Race Theory Is Not

"Critical race theory" has become a catch-all phrase among legislators attempting to ban a wide array of teaching practices concerning race. State legislators in Arizona, Arkansas, Idaho, Missouri, North Carolina, Oklahoma, South Carolina, Texas and West Virginia have introduced legislation banning what they believe to be critical race theory from schools.

But what is being banned in education, and what many media outlets and legislators are calling "critical race theory," is far from it. Here are sections from identical legislation in Oklahoma and Tennessee that propose to ban the teaching of these concepts. As a philosopher of race and racism, I can safely say that critical race theory does not assert the following:

(1) One race or sex is inherently superior to another race or sex;

(2) An individual, by virtue of the individual's race or sex, is inherently privileged, racist, sexist, or oppressive, whether consciously or subconsciously;

(3) An individual should be discriminated against or receive adverse treatment because of the individual's race or sex;

(4) An individual's moral character is determined by the individual's race or sex;

(5) An individual, by virtue of the individual's race or sex, bears responsibility for actions committed in the past by other members of the same race or sex;

(6) An individual should feel discomfort, guilt, anguish, or another form of psychological distress solely because of the individual's race or sex.

What most of these bills go on to do is limit the presentation of educational materials that suggest that Americans do not live in a meritocracy, that foundational elements of U.S. laws are racist, and that racism is a perpetual struggle from which America has not escaped.

Americans are used to viewing their history through a triumphalist lens, where we overcome hardships, defeat our British oppressors and create a country where all are free with equal access to opportunities.

Obviously, not all of that is true.

Critical race theory provides techniques to analyze U.S. history and legal institutions by acknowledging that racial problems do not go away when we leave them unaddressed.

> *"Sociologists and other scholars have long noted that racism can exist without racists."*

Racism Must Be Confronted

Rashawn Ray and Alexandra Gibbons

In the following viewpoint, Rashawn Ray and Alexandra Gibbons look at why critical race theory has become such a flash point for controversy in contemporary America. Critical race theory, the authors explain, examines how racism functions to oppress minorities in the criminal justice system, education system, labor market, housing market, and health care system, among others. CRT is not, however, concerned with individual racism. Those who object to its principles cannot make the distinction between underlying systems and personal bias and react as if they have been personally attacked. Efforts to ban the teaching of CRT are misguided, Ray and Gibbons write. If we love America, they say, we should seek to make it a better place for all. Rashawn Ray is senior fellow, governance studies, at the Brookings Institution and professor of sociology at the University of Maryland. Alexandra Gibbons is a research intern at the Brookings Institution.

"Why Are States Banning Critical Race Theory?" by Rashawn Ray and Alexandra Gibbons, The Brookings Institution, August 2021. Reprinted by permission.

As you read, consider the following questions:

1. Why have school boards and states across the country sought to ban critical race theory?
2. What are some examples of this practice?
3. According to the authors, how has neglecting racial studies affected school children?

Fox News has mentioned "critical race theory" 1,300 times in less than four months. Why? Because critical race theory (CRT) has become a new boogie man for people unwilling to acknowledge our country's racist history and how it impacts the present.

To understand why CRT has become such a flash point in the culture, it is important to understand what it is and what it is not. Opponents fear that CRT admonishes all white people for being oppressors while classifying all Black people as hopelessly oppressed victims. These fears have spurred school boards and state legislatures from Tennessee to Idaho to ban teachings about racism in classrooms. However, there is a fundamental problem: these narratives about CRT are gross exaggerations of the theoretical framework. The broad brush that is being applied to CRT is puzzling to academics, including some of the scholars who coined and advanced the framework.

CRT does not attribute racism to white people as individuals or even to entire groups of people. Simply put, critical race theory states that U.S. social institutions (e.g., the criminal justice system, education system, labor market, housing market, and healthcare system) are laced with racism embedded in laws, regulations, rules, and procedures that lead to differential outcomes by race. Sociologists and other scholars have long noted that racism can exist without racists. However, many Americans are not able to separate their individual identity as an American from the social institutions that govern us—these people perceive themselves as the system. Consequently, they interpret calling social institutions racist as calling them racist personally. It speaks to how normative racial ideology is to American identity that some people just cannot separate the two. There are also people who may recognize America's racist past but have bought into the false narrative that the U.S. is now an equitable democracy. They are simply unwilling to remove the blind spot obscuring the fact that America is still not great for everyone.

Scholars and activists who discuss CRT are not arguing that white people living now are to blame for what people did in the past. They are saying that white people living now have a moral responsibility to do something about how racism still impacts all of our lives today. Policies attempting to suffocate this much-needed national conversation are an obstacle to the pursuit of an equitable democracy. Supporters of CRT bans often quote Martin Luther King Jr's proclamation that individuals should be viewed by the content of their character instead of the color of their skin, ignoring the context of the quote and the true meaning behind it.

To better understand how widespread these efforts are to ban critical race theory from U.S. classrooms, we did an assessment of anti-CRT state legislation. Here's what we found:

- Eight states (Idaho, Oklahoma, Tennessee, Texas, Iowa, New Hampshire, Arizona, and South Carolina) have passed legislation.
- None of the state bills that have passed even actually mention the words "critical race theory" explicitly, with the exception of Idaho.
- The legislations mostly ban the discussion, training, and/or orientation that the U.S. is inherently racist as well as any discussions about conscious and unconscious bias, privilege, discrimination, and oppression. These parameters also extend beyond race to include gender lectures and discussions.
- State actors in Montana and South Dakota have denounced teaching concepts associated with CRT. The state school boards in Florida, Georgia, Utah, and Oklahoma introduced new guidelines barring CRT-related discussions. Local school

boards in Georgia, North Carolina, Kentucky, and Virginia also criticized CRT.

• Nearly 20 additional states have introduced or plan to introduce similar legislation.

The approach of some Republican-led state legislatures is a method for continuing to roll back racial progress regarding everything from voting rights to police reform. This is a horrible idea and does an injustice to our kids. Laws forbidding any teacher or lesson from mentioning race/racism, and even gender/sexism, would put a chilling effect on what educators are willing to discuss in the classroom and provide cover for those who are not comfortable hearing or telling the truth about the history and state of race relations in the United States. Ironically, "making laws outlawing critical race theory confirms the point that racism is embedded in the law," as sociologist Victor Ray noted.

Some parents are worried about their kids learning things in school that they do not have the capacity to address. As a college professor who does teach CRT as one of the many theoretical frameworks that I bring into the classroom, students are alarmed by how little they have learned about inequality. They are upset at their schools, teachers, and even their parents. So, this is the conundrum: teachers in K-12 schools are not actually teaching CRT. But teachers are trying to respond to students asking them why people are protesting and why Black people are more likely to be killed by the police.

Ultimately, we cannot employ colorblind ideology in a society that is far from colorblind. Everyone sees it, whether they acknowledge it consciously or not. As I wrote in a previous Brookings article on whether the U.S. is a racist country, systemic racism can explain racial disparities in police killings, COVID-19, and the devaluing of homes in Black neighborhoods. If we love America, we should want it to be the best it can be. Rather than run from the issue of racism in America, we should confront it head on. Our kids and country will be better for it.

*"We have already fought segregation
in the Civil War. We have already
gone through the Civil Rights
Movement. Critical race theory will
create more racism and segregation."*

The National Conversation on Race Shows No Sign of Ending

Kenny Cooper

In the following viewpoint, Kenny Cooper discusses how the national conversation about race has permeated one Pennsylvania school district. Although the district is 20% minority, only whites were among those speaking about race at a school board meeting. A local group has railed against the teaching of critical race theory, the 1619 Project, and other racially charged curricula, even though no district teachers are currently teaching CRT. The group believes that teaching CRT would be promoting radical racial theories. Other parents, fewer in number, have formed to push for an open dialogue. Kenny Cooper is a suburban reporter covering Montgomery and Delaware Counties for WHYY, a National Public Radio affiliate.

"The National Argument over Critical Race Theory Reaches Souderton School District," by WHYY, Inc./Kenny Cooper, June 18, 2021. Reprinted by permission.

As you read, consider the following questions:

1. Why do those in Soudy Strong Conservatives oppose teaching about race?
2. What other issues does this group support?
3. How do minority students fare academically versus their white counterparts in the Souderton Area School district?

I t was unclear just how many members of the community were packed into the high school cafeteria, but for those watching the Souderton Area School Board's meeting virtually on Zoom, the room felt shoulder-to-shoulder, based on the constant roar of applause and intermittent shouts from the audience.

IS THE 1619 PROJECT REWRITING HISTORY?

Confidence in institutions declines when they imprudently enlarge their missions. Empty pews rebuke churches that subordinate pastoral to political concerns. Prestige flows away from universities that prefer indoctrination to instruction. And trust evaporates when journalistic entities embrace political projects. On Monday, however, the *New York Times*—technically, one of its writers—received a Pulitzer Prize for just such an embrace.

Last August, an entire *Times* Sunday magazine was devoted to the multiauthor "1619 Project," whose proposition—subsequently developed in many other articles and multimedia content, and turned into a curriculum for schools—is that the nation's real founding was the arrival of 20 slaves in Virginia in 1619: The nation is about racism. Because the *Times* ignored today's most eminent relevant scholars—e.g., Brown University's Gordon Wood, Princeton's James McPherson and Sean Wilentz and Allen Guelzo, City University of New York's James Oakes, Columbia's Barbara Fields—the project's hectoring tone and ideological ax-grinding are unsurprising. Herewith three examples of slovenliness, even meretriciousness, regarding facts:

To establish that the American Revolution was launched to protect slavery, the *Times*'s project asserts that a November 1775 British

Though it was difficult to say what the headcount was, some word counts were possible. The word "equity" was mentioned 92 times. The word "race" and its various forms, 57 times. The word "white," 51 times.

The way the words were used spoke volumes.

"I've been told I'm white. But when I compare my skin tone to this white sheet of paper, it's obvious that I am not white on the color spectrum. White means no color, and I do not, in fact, know or have ever seen any people of no color or white. We are all people of color," said Jeanne Haynes of Green Lane.

"Critical race theory is no joke. These folks want us to pay them to train our teachers to see how irredeemably racist they and we all are," Haynes told the crowd in the cafeteria.

offer of freedom to slaves fleeing to join the British army was decisive in the move to independence. But this offer was a response to the war that had been boiling since April's battles at Lexington and Concord and simmering for a year before that, as detailed in Mary Beth Norton's just-published *1774: The Long Year of Revolution*.

Misdescribing an 1862 White House meeting with African American leaders, the project falsely says that President Abraham Lincoln flatly "opposed black equality" and adamantly favored colonization of emancipated slaves. Actually, Lincoln had already decided on an Emancipation Proclamation with no imperative of colonization. In Lincoln's final speech, his openness to black enfranchisement infuriated a member of his audience: John Wilkes Booth.

The project asserts that in the long struggle for freedom and civil rights, "for the most part" blacks fought "alone." This erases from history the important participation of whites, assiduously enlisted by, among others, Frederick Douglass and the Rev. Martin Luther King Jr.

The project's purpose is to displace the nation's actual 1776 founding, thereby draining from America's story the moral majesty of the first modern nation's Enlightenment precepts proclaimed in the Declaration of Independence and implemented by the Constitution.

"Opinion: The '1619 Project' Is Filled with Slovenliness and Ideological Ax-Grinding," by George F. Will., *Washington Post*, May 6, 2020.

The often-fiery national argument over critical race theory and the 1619 Project flared once again in the Philadelphia area Thursday night in Souderton, at a meeting that lasted roughly three hours.

The school district serves several of Montgomery County's smaller towns: Souderton and Telford boroughs, and Franconia, Lower Salford, Salford and Upper Salford townships. But the nationwide debate over race and anti-racism exists no matter a community's population.

And just as in other places across the United States, the issue didn't appear out of thin air at the Souderton School Board meeting. It was the culmination of a year of boiling frustration, claims of bigotry, and clashes among parents, school board members, and the community at large.

Add in a fast-approaching school board race with four seats up for grabs.

"We are all free and created equal. People have already fought bloody, horrific wars to protect our freedoms to fight for equality for all men and women. We have already fought segregation in the Civil War. We have already gone through the Civil Rights Movement. Critical race theory will create more racism and segregation," said Becky Phipps of Telford.

Critical race theory is not a new school curriculum by any means. It is a decades-old framework that was conceptualized in the 1970s and 1980s by legal scholars Derrick Bell, Kimberlé Williams Crenshaw, and Patricia Williams, among others.

The basic idea is that race is a social construct that permeates many aspects of life in the United States, such as the legal system and social structures—and that racism is a systemic issue, not an individual one. Though critical race theory was initially designed to inform the field of law, it expanded into areas of academia.

Currently, critical race theory is sometimes used in college-level legal studies courses and other academic areas, but not typically in first-grade classrooms. But that hasn't stopped it from being vilified by people who take issue with diversity, inclusion, and anti-racism efforts.

Conservative state legislatures across the country have drafted legislation against the teaching of critical race theory and the 1619 Project in schools—a move that some educators fear will be used to prevent them from teaching about racism and the history of the country. (How, for example, the Civil War was about slavery, not segregation. Though discussed before the Civil War, segregation was a postwar phenomenon.)

Souderton School Board President Ken Keith appeared to tip his hand on the issue at the start of the meeting.

"Other topics have been thrusted into the forefront of national discussions and have made their way into all communities. I would like to be clear on two of these topics. In Souderton, we are not following or teaching critical race theory in our schools, any more than we are following—" Keith said as the crowd interrupted him with a 30-second round of applause.

He finished his thought by likening critical race theory to communism and said that it may only be mentioned in discussion.

"In addition, on the topic of implicit bias training, the Souderton Area School District is not mandating or funding this training," Keith said. "… In short, we will not allow a political agenda to dictate a departure from what we know to be a solid successful educational practice that has served our students well."

Keith concluded his opening remarks by acknowledging that the district would be undergoing "a comprehensive planning process which is required by the Pennsylvania Department of Education every three years," and that in this process, equity will be examined.

WHYY News reached out to Keith as well as several others in leadership positions at the school district, but did not receive responses.

Problem Conversations

Richard Detwiler, a retired teacher, did not speak during the board meeting, but he said he is concerned about the area where he sent his now-adult children to school. He said that the group of parents opposed to teaching about race and racism in schools has latched onto words and phrases like critical race theory as a "source of divisiveness and negativity."

"I'm really sort of surprised and shocked by the very loud voices, both nationally and locally here in the community, that have a problem with those conversations and want to call them un-American and unpatriotic," Detwiler said.

He went to the board meeting in person to observe the back-and-forth, but Detwiler said it is far from novel.

Shortly after the police killing of George Floyd last June in Minneapolis, the Souderton area, like many other places, looked in the mirror for a reckoning. A local activist with the Movement for Black and Brown Lives in Montgomery County organized a "well-attended" march.

And though many were complacent with the status quo, some community members were not and urged the school district to address equity concerns. Not long after the appeal from community members, Superintendent Frank Gallagher wrote a letter regarding equity in the Souderton Area School District.

"We unequivocally condemn acts of race-based violence and any intolerant rhetoric which seeks to divide us. In SASD, we actively work to build an inclusive school community that values diversity, and we stand united against hate in any form," Gallagher wrote.

In the letter, Gallagher announced the creation of an equity committee "to examine these issues and to develop a comprehensive action plan with the input of stakeholders across our community."

A year later, the concerned parents are still waiting to learn the findings of the committee. And since last June, community relations have grown more hostile. The school board has barred Carmina Taylor, a co-founder of the Movement for Black and Brown Lives in Montgomery County, from speaking during their meetings. They say it's because she doesn't live in the district.

According to Detwiler, the committee was supposed to engage in the so-called "equity audit" this summer—which set off the alarms among conservative parents already amped up by the coming school board election.

"We can't really know to what extent our schools, for example, are the safe and welcoming places that we would like them to be and that we think they are, without doing the kind of equity audit that has been proposed and ostensibly planned to begin this summer," Detwiler said.

Roughly 80% of the Souderton Area School District's nearly 6,500 students are white.

A collection of parents formed a Facebook group called Soudy Strong Conservatives at the end of March. WHYY News requested access to the group to speak with some of its nearly 450 members, but has not been allowed in. However, this statement appears on the group's "about" page.

"This group is for conservatives in the Souderton Area School District who stand with the Souderton School Board in preserving the traditional educational model that raises proud Americans. We support full-time in-person education and stand against radical ideology such as The 1619 Project, Critical Race Theory, and Comprehensive Sexuality Education. Let's let kids be kids and academics be academics … and let's leave politics and gender studies to the collegiate levels.

#andYESweareforUNMASKINGourchildrentoo!"

WHYY News was able to get in contact with Dana Vesey, a Souderton parent with two middle schoolers. She is one of the three administrators of the Soudy Strong Conservatives Facebook group.

She characterized the last year in Souderton and the buzz around the school board as an example of politicization. She said that organizing through school boards is just the accessible way to address concerns that are "bigger as a whole with the movement of the country."

Vesey said she couldn't speak for the Soudy Strong Conservative group, since it was formed by Kaitlin Derstine, a parent actively involved with the Parents For In Person Education group in Montgomery County.

But Vesey did offer her perspective on the critical race theory debate.

"I do not believe in these mass teachings of things like critical race theory, or anything that's going to result in critical race theory. I'm not sold that they are a proven positive solution," Vesey said.

Dru Shelly, a Harleysville parent, said she was shocked to see the formation of such a group. She sees many of the members at church, softball, and other community events.

"It just breaks my heart that they are so afraid for their kids that they can't open themselves up to a different perspective," Shelly said.

She attributed the strong opinions to a lack of factual information. Though Shelly does hold the opposing parents accountable for their own viewpoints, she pointed the finger more at the school board, which she said has been unable to stay unbiased.

"The board has their own ideas that they discuss amongst themselves, and their supporters are quite loud and their supporters are welcome to come to the meeting and say whatever they'd like in front of the camera, including giving advice on who to vote for in the upcoming election," Shelly said.

Motivated to stop the conservative group of parents, other parents created a Facebook group called SASD Parents for Unity in May. The group has amassed a membership of more than 100 people, though they are largely outnumbered by the opposing faction.

Parent Stephanie Jamison, a founding member of the group, believes the situation in the school district is a cause for concern.

"As I've been engaging and organizing in this community, I've received countless phone calls from families telling me their firsthand experiences with the school districts and in our schools and their heartbreaking stories. And people are scared of intimidation, they're scared of violence for speaking out," Jamison said.

She pointed to a well-documented growing achievement and disciplinary gap in Souderton as a reason why an equity audit is needed.

Spurred to Action

According to a 2021 report from Public Citizens for Children and Youth, there was a more than 25% reading and math score gap between Black and Hispanic students and their white counterparts in Souderton district schools. ProPublica's Miseducation project found large gaps in opportunity, discipline, and achievement between students of color and white students in Souderton schools.

Jamison said the data shocked her into action. She said that previous conversations regarding educational equity were squashed, and that the board's barring of Carmina Taylor as a speaker helped inspire the formation of the new Facebook group.

"I was ashamed of how they were treating this woman from the community who's really invested in educational equity and who has expertise and information to share with us. And she was being obstructed from participating," Jamison said.

Jamison credited Taylor and other members of her group for bringing issues regarding educational equity to light.

Taylor was present during Thursday night's school board meeting and said she has been barred three times from speaking. Though the board says that's because she is not a resident of the district, Taylor pointed to its policy manual, which states, "The Board requires that public participants be residents of this district or anyone having registered a legitimate interest in a contemplated action of the Board; anyone representing a group in the community or school district…"

Because Taylor represents a countywide organization and several community members permitted her to speak on their behalf, she believes that she is qualified to speak. A petition to allow her to speak at a previous school board meeting had 40 community signatures.

During Thursday's meeting, a group of parents led by Kaitlin Derstine, of Soudy Strong Conservatives, led an 18-minute charge against Taylor, critical race theory, and any talks regarding equity.

Even though speakers were supposed to be limited to 3-minute comments, Derstine's remarks were allowed to be read in their entirety as long as other parents picked up and read from where the last one left off.

Reading from Derstine's written comments, one parent in the group, Ashley Peterson of Harleysville, attempted to address the achievement gap by making generalizations about the Black community.

"As for our African American community, I found that it can be culturally normative to start their children in school in first grade, which can put them a year or two behind other children. Many have also moved here more recently from the city, which is coming from a different school system that has different standards. So this gap in test scores is very easily answered without an equity audit," Peterson said.

When Derstine's last surrogate finished speaking, the cafeteria broke out into another round of applause.

In an interview, Taylor accused School Board President Keith of creating a combative environment with his opening speech.

"When have you ever heard a school board president open a meeting like that? Why would he do that?" Taylor asked.

Critical race theory is not taught in K-12 Souderton classrooms and no one at the meeting proposed that it should be. Taylor said she believes that the parents speaking out against her were using rhetoric designed to cloud judgment. Taylor added, however, that she was able to have positive discussions with Vesey of the Soudy Strong Conservatives before Thursday night.

Parents at the Podium

Throughout the more than three-hour-long meeting, parents from both groups came to the podium and delivered remarks to the audience.

Noah Bass of Lower Salford said his daughter was the victim of antisemitism in the district. Though he extended his thanks to staff members who advocated for his daughter, he had tough questions for the district regarding the perceived lack of attention being brought to the issue as a whole.

"We're also aware that the undercurrent of racism and intolerance that exists in our schools has been getting worse. Worsening patterns of overt usage of hate speech, derogatory slurs, and symbols of hate are fueled by students' unchecked behavior. Throughout this entire school year, we have heard our kids tell us how commonly racist and homophobic slurs are whispered, spoken, and screened in the classrooms, hallways, and school buses of our school district, and nothing is done about it," Bass said.

Charl Wilner said she found it "interesting" that an all-white school board and a nearly all-white audience was having a conversation about race and "saying, 'Wow, I have no idea what anybody's talking about.'"

She accused board members of being obtuse and said they had no interest in teaching an increasingly diverse student body about the "real honest history" of the United States.

In an interview prior to the school board meeting, parent Stephanie Jamison also zeroed in on a changing America—and a changing Souderton, and why she believes the board has to do more if it wants to serve the entire community.

"I think a frequent comment I've heard from the school board is, 'We know that demographics are shifting.' But the reality is the demographics started shifting like 40 years ago. And like, I'm not sure how much they have to shift before they realize that, you know, there are people of color in our community, and we need to be intentional about making this community inclusive and safe for everyone," Jamison said.

Though the meeting came to a conclusion—or rather, went into an extended recess—parents from both groups don't expect the issues to go away anytime soon. There are school board seats in play, and a national conversion that shows no signs of ending.

Periodical and Internet Sources Bibliography

The following articles have been selected to supplement the diverse views presented in this chapter.

Jelani Cobb, "The Man Behind Critical Race Theory," *New Yorker*, September 13, 2021, https://www.newyorker.com/magazine /2021/09/20/the-man-behind-critical-race-theory.

"Editorial: The '1619 Project' Is Bad History Fueled by Bad Motives," *Washington Times*, May 24, 2020, https://www.washingtontimes .com/news/2020/may/24/editorial-1619-project-bad-history -fueled-bad-moti/.

Jacey Fortin, "Critical Race Theory: A Brief History," *New York Times*, November 8, 2021, https://www.nytimes.com/article/what-is -critical-race-theory.html.

Janel George, "A Lesson on Critical Race Theory," American Bar Association, January 11, 2021, https://www.americanbar.org /groups/crsj/publications/human_rights_magazine_home/civil -rights-reimagining-policing/a-lesson-on-critical-race-theory/.

Leslie M. Harris, "I Helped Fact-Check the 1619 Project. The *Times* Ignored Me," Politico, March 6, 2020, https://www.politico.com /news/magazine/2020/03/06/1619-project-new-york-times -mistake-122248.

Shannon Keating. "One Small Town's Big Battle Over Critical Race Theory," Buzzfeed News, November 1, 2021, https://www .buzzfeednews.com/article/shannonkeating/critical-race-theory -guilford-school-board-elections.

Timothy Sandefur, "The 1619 Project: An Autopsy," Cato Institute, October 27, 2020, https://www.cato.org/commentary/1619 -project-autopsy.

Stephen Sawchuck, "What Is Critical Race Theory, and Why Is It Under Attack?" *Education Week*, May 18, 2021, https://www .edweek.org/leadership/what-is-critical-race-theory-and-why-is -it-under-attack/2021/05.

Adam Serwer, "The Fight Over the 1619 Project Is Not About the Facts," *The Atlantic*, December 23, 2019, https://www .theatlantic.com/ideas/archive/2019/12/historians-clash-1619 -project/604093/.

CHAPTER 3

Should Social Media Be Censored?

Chapter Preface

P rotests erupted in the wake of the 2020 killing of George Floyd at the hands of police on the streets of Minneapolis, Minnesota. Most were peaceful, but there are always bad actors in any group, and looting and other crimes occurred as well. It was then that former president Donald Trump tweeted his now infamous response: "When the looting starts, the shooting starts."

After this tweet, Facebook saw a drastic increase in user hate speech and threats of violence. It was not until the infamous Capitol riot on January 6, 2021, however, that a lame duck Trump was banned from social media sites such as Twitter and Facebook.

Hate speech is egregious, and most users would agree that it should be eliminated. But what about less harmful but still deleterious forms of communication, such as misinformation— whether deliberate or unintentional? During a pandemic, for instance, such misinformation can be deadly.

Despite the banning of a president, misinformation, hate speech, and other information inimical to public welfare has persisted on the internet. Facebook, for one, has been cited as a platform that has had malignant effects both in the United States and abroad. The January 6 insurrection at the US Capitol was facilitated, at least in part, by information spread over Facebook and other social media.

In countries such as India, lax oversight by Facebook allegedly allowed hate speech and disinformation that led to political violence. This paradigm has replicated itself in country after country where Facebook operates. And according to the news magazine *The Week*, Facebook employees were horrified by their complicity in fomenting anger and hatred worldwide. They spoke up to their supervisors, to no avail, because Facebook founder and CEO Mark Zuckerberg chose not to heed their warnings. According to employees, he prized reader engagement and advertising revenue above all else.

A Facebook whistleblower, Frances Haugen, came forward with accusations that the social media site used algorithms that promoted and rewarded anger and hatred. She released a trove of reports, memos, discussion threads, and other documents that supported her claims. In response, Zuckerberg stated that the news coverage that followed was "a coordinated effort to selectively use leaked documents to create a false picture about our company."

His employees had a different opinion. "Hey, we're actively making the world worse, FYI," one wrote. "History will not judge us kindly." Those are strong words, but the truth is that Facebook, Twitter, Instagram, Tik Tok, and the like wield extraordinary power in society today, when tweets and Facebook posts are literally matters of life and death.

But the answer to social media's sins is not as simple as enacting censorship. Despite spending millions, social media companies such as Twitter and Facebook are nearly helpless in patrolling the vast number of posts on their sites and weeding out hatred and lies. The question we may well ask is not whether censorship is desirable or not, but if it is even possible on today's internet. Facebook whistleblower Sophie Zhang has compared attempting to police social media "to trying to empty the ocean with a colander."

Social media moguls such as Zuckerberg may not be doing all they can to counteract internet ills, but it would likely take a campaign far in excess of anything ever attempted to make social media a safe environment for all.

| "The consequences of believing that vaccines cause harm are eminently more dangerous than believing that the earth is flat. The former creates serious public health problems, the latter makes for a good laugh at a bar."

Social Media Platforms Should Take Responsibility for the Content They Publish

Niam Yaraghi

In the following viewpoint, Niam Yaraghi discusses the proliferation of misinformation and hate speech on social media and considers alternatives for combating these scourges. The sheer number of posts on social media, millions and millions per day, prevents platforms from using a human response. Yaraghi suggests a combination of human decisions that will inform algorithms designed to tackle hate speech and misinformation. He discusses two methods of handling such posts, videos, and the like. The first is to delete them. The second is to provide links so that viewers may access correct information and educate themselves. Niam Yaraghi is assistant professor of business technology at Miami Herbert Business School at the University of Miami and a nonresident senior fellow at the Brookings Institution's Center for Technology Innovation.

"How Should Social Media Platforms Combat Misinformation and Hate Speech?" by Niam Yaraghi, The Brookings Institution, April 9, 2019. Reprinted by permission.

As you read, consider the following questions:

1. What are two ways to view social media platforms with regard to their content?
2. Why must social media companies rely in part on their communities to report objectionable material?
3. Why does the author prefer providing alternative, correct information to outright censorship?

Social media companies are under increased scrutiny for their mishandling of hateful speech and fake news on their platforms. There are two ways to consider a social media platform: On one hand, we can view them as technologies that merely enable individuals to publish and share content, a figurative blank sheet of paper on which anyone can write anything. On the other hand, one can argue that social media platforms have now evolved into curators of content. I argue that these companies should take some responsibility over the content that is published on their platforms and suggest a set of strategies to help them with dealing with fake news and hate speech.

Artificial and Human Intelligence Together

At the beginning, social media companies established themselves not to hold any accountability over the content being published on their platforms. In the intervening years, they have since set up a mix of automated and human driven editorial processes to promote or filter certain types of content. In addition to that, their users are increasingly using these platforms as the primary source of getting their news. Twitter moments, in which you can see a brief snapshot of the daily news, is a prime example of how Twitter is getting closer to becoming a news media. As social media practically become news media, their level of responsibility over the content which they distribute should increase accordingly.

While I believe it is naïve to consider social media as merely neutral content sharing technologies with no responsibility, I do not believe that we should either have the same level of editorial expectation from social media that we have from traditional news media.

The sheer volume of content shared on social media makes it impossible to establish a comprehensive editorial system. Take Twitter as an example: It is estimated that 500 million tweets are sent per day. Assuming that each tweet contains 20 words on average, the volume of content published on Twitter in one single day will be equivalent to that of the *New York Times* in 182 years. The terminology and focus of the hate speech changes over time, and most fake news articles contain some level of truthfulness in them. Therefore, social media companies cannot solely rely on artificial intelligence or humans to monitor and edit their content. They should rather develop approaches that utilize artificial and human intelligence together.

Finding the Needle in a Haystack

To overcome the editorial challenges of so much content, I suggest that the companies focus on a limited number of topics which are deemed important with significant consequences. The anti-vaccination movement and those who believe in flat-earth theory are both spreading anti-scientific and fake content. However, the consequences of believing that vaccines cause harm are eminently more dangerous than believing that the earth is flat. The former creates serious public health problems, the latter makes for a good laugh at a bar. Social media companies should convene groups of experts in various domains to constantly monitor the major topics in which fake news or hate speech may cause serious harm.

It is also important to consider how recommendation algorithms on social media platforms may inadvertently promote fake and hateful speech. At their core, these recommendation systems group users based on their shared interests and then promote the same type of content to all users within each group. If most of the users in one group have interests in, say, flat-earth theory and anti-vaccination hoaxes, then the algorithm will promote the anti-vaccination content to the users in the same group who may only be interested in flat-earth theory. Over time, the exposure to such promoted content could persuade the users who initially believed in vaccines to become skeptical about them. Once the major areas of focus for combating the fake and hateful speech is determined, the social media companies can tweak their recommendation systems fairly easily so that they will not nudge users to the harmful content.

Once those limited number of topics are identified, social media companies should decide on how to fight the spread of such content. In rare instances, the most appropriate response is to censor and ban the content with no hesitation. Examples include posts that incite violence or invite others to commit crimes. The recent New Zealand incident in which the shooter live broadcasted his heinous crimes on Facebook is the prime example of the content which should have never been allowed to be posted and shared on the platform.

Facebook currently relies on its community of users to flag such content and then uses an army of real humans to monitor such content within 24 hours to determine if they are actually in violation of its terms of use. Live content is monitored by humans once it reaches a certain level of popularity. While it is easier to use artificial intelligence to monitor textual content in real-time, our technologies to analyze images and videos are quickly advancing. For example, Yahoo! has recently made its algorithms to detect offensive and adult images public. The AI algorithms of Facebook are getting smart enough to detect and flag non-consensual intimate images.

Fight Misinformation with Information

Currently, social media companies have adopted two approaches to fight misinformation. The first one is to block such content outright. For example, Pinterest bans anti-vaccination content and Facebook bans white supremacist content. The other is to provide alternative information alongside the content with fake information so that the users are exposed to the truth and correct information. This approach, which is implemented by YouTube, encourages users to click on the links with verified and vetted information that would debunk the misguided claims made in fake or hateful content. If you search "Vaccines cause autism" on YouTube, while you still can view the videos posted by anti-vaxxers, you will also be presented with a link to the Wikipedia page of MMR vaccine that debunks such beliefs.

While we yet have to empirically examine and compare the effectiveness of these alternative approaches, I prefer to present users with the real information and allow them to become informed and willfully abandon their misguided beliefs by exposing them to the reliable sources of information. Regardless of their short-lived impact, diversity of ideas will ultimately move us forward by enriching our discussions. Social media companies will be able to censor content online, but they cannot control how ideas spread offline. Unless individuals are presented with counter arguments, falsehoods and hateful ideas will spread easily, as they have in the past when social media did not exist.

> "For researchers, isolating the effect
> of misinformation is thus extremely
> challenging. It's not often that a
> user will share both accurate and
> inaccurate information about
> the same event, and at nearly the
> same time."

What to Do About Misinformation
on Social Media

Chris Meserole

In the following viewpoint, Chris Meserole discusses the proliferation of misinformation on social media. In particular, he cites one incident in which a domestic terrorist killed nine people in Toronto. Meserole notes that a journalist sent out two competing tweets in the immediate aftermath regarding the shooter's identity. The incorrect tweet went viral, while its accurate counterpart did not. Misinformation spread due to the biases of readers. The author argues that social media companies need to develop methods to deal with blatantly incorrect information, as in this case. Chris Meserole is a fellow in foreign policy at the Brookings Institution and director of research for the Brookings Artificial Intelligence and Emerging Technology Initiative. He is also an adjunct professor at Georgetown University.

"How Misinformation Spreads on Social Media—and What to Do About It," by Chris Meserole, The Brookings Institution, May 9, 2018. Reprinted by permission.

As you read, consider the following questions:

1. Why, according to Meserole, is determining the effect of misinformation difficult?
2. How did Twitter change its algorithm, and what effect did this change have?
3. What are some solutions to the misinformation problem that Meserole discusses?

W e take misinformation seriously," Facebook CEO Mark Zuckerberg wrote just weeks after the 2016 election. In the year since, the question of how to counteract the damage done by "fake news" has become a pressing issue both for technology companies and governments across the globe.

Yet as widespread as the problem is, opportunities to glimpse misinformation in action are fairly rare. Most users who generate misinformation do not share accurate information too, so it can be difficult to tease out the effect of misinformation itself. For example, when President Trump shares misinformation on Twitter, his tweets tend to go viral. But they may not be going viral because of the misinformation: All those retweets may instead owe to the popularity of Trump's account, or the fact that he writes about politically charged subjects. Without a corresponding set of accurate tweets from Trump, there's no way of knowing what role misinformation is playing.

For researchers, isolating the effect of misinformation is thus extremely challenging. It's not often that a user will share both accurate and inaccurate information about the same event, and at nearly the same time.

Yet shortly after the recent attack in Toronto, that is exactly what a CBC journalist did. In the chaotic aftermath of the attack, Natasha Fatah published two competing eyewitness accounts: one (wrongly, as it turned out) identifying the attacker as "angry" and "Middle Eastern," and another correctly identifying him as "white."

Fatah's tweets are by no means definitive, but they do represent a natural experiment of sorts. And the results show just how fast misinformation can travel. The initial tweet—which wrongly identified the attacker as Middle Eastern—received far more engagement than the accurate one in the roughly five hours after the attack.

Worse, the tweet containing correct information did not perform much better over a longer time horizon, up to 24 hours after the attack.

Taken together, Fatah's tweets suggest that misinformation on social media genuinely is a problem. As such, they raise two questions: First, why did the incorrect tweet spread so much faster than the correct one? And second, what can be done to prevent the similar spread of misinformation in the future?

The Speed of Misinformation on Twitter

For most of Twitter's history, its newsfeed was straightforward: The app showed tweets in reverse chronological order. That changed in 2015 with the introduction of Twitter's algorithmic newsfeed, which displayed tweets based on a calculation of "relevance" rather than recency.

Last year, the company's engineering team revealed how its current algorithm works. As with Facebook and YouTube, Twitter now relies on a deep learning algorithm that has learned to prioritize content with greater prior engagement. By combing through Twitter's data, the algorithm has taught itself that Twitter users are more likely to stick around if they see content that has already gotten a lot of retweets and mentions, compared with content that has fewer.

The flow of misinformation on Twitter is thus a function of both human and technical factors. Human biases play an important role: Since we're more likely to react to content that taps into our existing grievances and beliefs, inflammatory tweets will generate quick engagement. It's only after that engagement happens that the technical side kicks in: If a tweet is retweeted, favorited, or replied to by enough of its first viewers, the newsfeed algorithm will show it to more users, at which point it will tap into the biases of those users too—prompting even more engagement, and so on. At its worse, this cycle can turn social media into a kind of confirmation bias machine, one perfectly tailored for the spread of misinformation.

If you look at Fatah's tweets, the process above plays out almost to a tee. A small subset of Fatah's followers immediately engaged with the tweet reporting a bystander's account of the attacker as "angry" and "Middle Eastern," which set off a cycle in which greater engagement begat greater viewership and vice versa. By contrast, the tweet that accurately identified the attacker received little initial engagement, was flagged less by the newsfeed algorithm, and thus never really caught on. The result was an exponential increase in engagement for the inaccurate tweet, but only a modest increase for the accurate one.

What to Do About It

Just as the problem has both a human and technical side, so too does any potential solution.

Where Twitter's algorithms are concerned, there is no shortage of low-hanging fruit. During an attack itself, Twitter could promote police or government accounts so that accurate information is disseminated as quickly as possible. Alternately, it could also display a warning at the top of its search and trending feeds about the unreliability of initial eyewitness accounts.

Even more, Twitter could update its "While You Were Away" and search features. In the case of the Toronto attack, Twitter could not have been expected to identify the truth faster than the Toronto police. But once the police had identified the attacker, Twitter should have had systems in place to restrict the visibility of Fatah's tweet and other trending misinformation. For example, over ten days after the attack, the top two results for a search of the attacker were these:

So a Muslim terrorist killed 9 people using a van. What else is new. Still wondering why the news was quick to mention it was a Ryder rental van but not the religion or this evil POS

Inclusive #Toronto will not allow a little thing like a Muslim mowing down and killing 9 people to divide it, those 9 died for the greater good. Kumbaya m*** f****.

(I conducted the above search while logged into my own Twitter account, but a search while logged out produced the same results.)

Unfortunately, these were not isolated tweets. Anyone using Twitter to follow and learn about the attack has been greeted with a wealth of misinformation and invective. This is something Twitter can combat: Either it can hire an editorial team to track and remove blatant misinformation from trending searches, or it can introduce a new reporting feature for users to flag misinformation as they come across it. Neither option is perfect, and the latter would not be trivial to implement. But the status quo is worse. How many Twitter users continue to think the Toronto attack was the work of Middle Eastern jihadists, and that Prime Minister Justin Trudeau's immigration policies are to blame?

Ultimately, however, the solution to misinformation will also need to involve the users themselves. Not only do Twitter's users need to better understand their own biases, but journalists in particular need to better understand how their mistakes can be exploited. In this case, the biggest errors were human ones: Fatah tweeted out an account without corroborating it, even though the eyewitness in question, a man named David Leonard, himself noted that "I can't confirm or deny whether my observation is correct."

To counter misinformation online, we can and should demand that newsfeed algorithms not amplify our worst instincts. But we can't expect them to save us from ourselves.

> *"Blocking out entire belief systems forces people to speak only amongst themselves, and thereby become more entrenched in what they believe."*

The Left Should Worry About Censorship

Julius E. Ewungkem

In the following viewpoint, Julius E. Ewungkem states that while he felt former US president Donald Trump's ban from social media was justified, the general implications of such a ban are worrisome. Social media companies, Ewungkem writes, hold great power over public discourse, yet their first priority is making money, not ensuring free speech. The practice of allowing opposing viewpoints, Ewungkem asserts, is a powerful one, and banning those who disagree can lead people to seek out echo chambers where everyone thinks the same way. It is much more beneficial in a society to promote an interchange of ideas where both sides can be heard. Julius E. Ewungkem is an opinion writer for The Harvard Crimson.

As you read, consider the following questions:

1. According to the author, why do social media companies have the right to ban users?
2. Why did conservatives flock to the social media site Parler?
3. According to Ewungkem, how can we as a society attempt to curtail polarization?

Over the past couple months, there has been an increasing amount of controversy concerning widespread Big Tech suppression. Many conservatives feel that their opinions are being stifled on the internet due to left-leaning bias within social media companies. To them, Donald Trump's ban from Twitter, Facebook, Instagram, Snapchat, and almost every other popular social media platform was extremely alarming. Personally, I felt a little torn about the event. Though I wholeheartedly think the removal was deserved and the majority of claims of the suppression of opinions is overblown, the underlying implications of the ban were somewhat worrying and highlight a growing issue of political division in our country.

Twitter, Facebook, and other large social media corporations each have the right to control who's allowed on their platform. They all have terms of service, and if they feel that an individual or group of individuals has violated those rules, they all reserve the right to ban those people from their platform. However, while these private companies are acting well within their rights, their platforms are critical areas for public discourse. Politicians use Twitter and Instagram to publish political statements and debate their fellow elected officials. By deciding who can and cannot speak, social media can effectively control the public narrative on many discussions.

Furthermore, these corporations' first priority isn't to create a perfect space for political discourse—it's their own profit margins. If these two goals happen to align, they'll act in a way that benefits all, but it might not always transpire that way. These companies haven't been "elected"; they have no democratic accountability, and so the public's well-being holds limited weight in their decisions.

In spite of this, it is a massive overreaction to call this extreme censorship. Trump, by the time he was removed from Twitter, had violated its terms of service multiple times. It also does not make sense to accuse these companies of collective censorship because this was an isolated incident; we haven't really seen anyone with such power silenced on such a large scale before.

Additionally, what would the alternative option even be? Would we rather have social media sites with no terms of service? Or have the government play a role in these forms of media? These are complicated questions to which we are still developing the answer. Ultimately, the more pressing issue is the growing aversion to open discussion.

Across social media, advocating for an unpopular standpoint or even just asking a question can garner massive amounts of hate, even if there was no malice intended. Such reactions ostracize opposing viewpoints and push people to congregate within echo chambers that magnify hate and mute dissent. We saw this with Parler, a social media platform that devolved into a place for extreme right-wingers to spread misinformation, form conspiracies, and even plan insurgencies. The app was filled with Proud Boys members, Holocaust deniers, and white supremacists. Yet, on Nov. 8, during the presidential election, the Parler app was among the most downloaded apps on the internet. And while some extremists might've joined the community to spread hate and conspiracies unchecked, I don't think that was the selling point for most people. The company framed itself as a place to "speak freely and express yourself openly without fear of being 'deplatformed' for your views," playing on the growing fear of cancel culture. And so people flocked to the app, exposing themselves to many of these insane theories and throwing themselves down this rabbit hole.

Now, I know it is a somewhat privileged idea to want to have these discussions, as not everyone wants to engage with opposing views, especially when sometimes it is their own existence that is being questioned. Additionally, not all opinions should have a platform. Some speech is just blatantly hateful or false, and this rhetoric should not have a place to exist. However, blocking out entire belief systems forces people to speak only amongst themselves, and thereby become more entrenched in what they believe.

As someone who leans heavily towards the left, this is the worst thing possible, as no change can occur until more of our voting population comes together on certain issues. There will always be those who don't listen, but we must strive to curb the trend of polarization. As Harvard students, we sometimes fall into this trap, forming our own echo chamber and not giving opposing views a place. Listening shouldn't come at the expense of one's mental health or well-being, and not everyone is open to discussion. But, if conceivable, instead of pushing a differing opinion away, we should try to spend some time understanding where the speaker is coming from and respectfully offer our own opinion as well.

> "Nine-in-ten Republicans and independents who lean toward the Republican Party say it's at least somewhat likely that social media platforms censor political viewpoints they find objectionable."

Americans Don't Trust Social Media Platforms

Emily A. Vogels, Andrew Perrin, and Monica Anderson

In the following viewpoint, Emily A. Vogels, Andrew Perrin, and Monica Anderson examine Americans' attitudes toward social media sites with regard to censorship. As expected, attitudes differ along partisan lines, but these differences are stark. Republican distrust of the media in general extends to social media, as a high percentage of right-leaning voters believes that social media companies lean left and that these companies regularly censor conservative voices. Democrats and those leaning left, by comparison, are more likely to trust social media companies, but even these citizens are generally skeptical that social media companies can be trusted. Monica Anderson is associate director of research at the Pew Research Center. Emily A. Vogels is a research associate, and Andrew Perrin is a research analyst there.

"Most Americans Think Social Media Sites Censor Political Viewpoints," by Emily A. Vogels, Andrew Perrin, and Monica Anderson, Pew Research Center, August 19, 2020. Reprinted by permission.

As you read, consider the following questions:

1. How do Americans feel about labeling politicians' posts as inaccurate?
2. How do Americans feel about labeling ordinary citizens' post as inaccurate?
3. How do opinions vary depending on one's political viewpoint?

Americans have complicated feelings about their relationship with big technology companies. While they have appreciated the impact of technology over recent decades and rely on these companies' products to communicate, shop and get news, many have also grown critical of the industry and have expressed concerns about the executives who run them.

This has become a particularly pointed issue in politics—with critics accusing tech firms of political bias and stifling open discussion. Amid these concerns, a Pew Research Center survey conducted in June finds that roughly three-quarters of U.S. adults say it is very (37%) or somewhat (36%) likely that social media sites intentionally censor political viewpoints that they find objectionable. Just 25% believe this is not likely the case.

Majorities in both major parties believe censorship is likely occurring, but this belief is especially common—and growing—among Republicans. Nine-in-ten Republicans and independents who lean toward the Republican Party say it's at least somewhat likely that social media platforms censor political viewpoints they find objectionable, up slightly from 85% in 2018, when the Center last asked this question.

At the same time, the idea that major technology companies back liberal views over conservative ones is far more widespread among Republicans. Today, 69% of Republicans and Republican leaners say major technology companies generally support the views of liberals over conservatives, compared with 25% of

Democrats and Democratic leaners. Again, these sentiments among Republicans have risen slightly over the past two years.

Debates about censorship grew earlier this summer following Twitter's decision to label tweets from President Donald Trump as misleading. This prompted some of the president's supporters to charge that these platforms are censoring conservative voices.

This survey finds that the public is fairly split on whether social media companies should engage in this kind of fact-checking, but there is little public confidence that these platforms could determine which content should be flagged.

Partisanship is a key factor in views about the issue. Fully 73% of Democrats say they strongly or somewhat approve of social media companies labeling posts on their platforms from elected officials as inaccurate or misleading. On the other hand, 71% of Republicans say they at least somewhat disapprove of this practice. Republicans are also far more likely than Democrats to say they have no confidence at all that social media companies would be able to determine which posts on their platforms should be labeled as inaccurate or misleading (50% vs. 11%).

These are among the key findings of a Pew Research Center survey of 4,708 U.S. adults conducted June 16-22, 2020, using the Center's American Trends Panel.

Views about whether social media companies should label posts on their platforms as inaccurate are sharply divided along political lines

Americans are divided over whether social media companies should label posts on their sites as inaccurate or misleading, with most being skeptical that these sites can accurately determine what content should be flagged.

Some 51% of Americans say they strongly or somewhat approve of social media companies labeling posts from elected officials on their platforms as inaccurate or misleading, while a similar share (46%) say they at least somewhat disapprove of this.

Democrats and Republicans hold contrasting views about the appropriateness of social media companies flagging inaccurate information on their platforms. Fully 73% of Democrats say they strongly or somewhat approve of social media companies labeling posts on their platforms from elected officials as inaccurate or misleading, versus 25% who disapprove.

These sentiments are nearly reversed for Republicans: 71% say they disapprove of social media companies engaging in this type of labeling, including about four-in-ten (39%) who say they strongly disapprove. Just 27% say they approve of this labeling.

Liberal Democrats stand out as being the most supportive of this practice: 85% of this group say they approve of social media companies labeling elected officials' posts as inaccurate or misleading, compared with 64% of conservative or moderate Democrats and even smaller shares of moderate or liberal Republicans and conservative Republicans (38% and 21%, respectively).

In addition to measuring public attitudes about flagging potentially misleading content from elected officials, the survey explored Americans' views about whether this practice would be acceptable to apply to posts from ordinary users. Some 52% of Americans say they strongly or somewhat approve of social media companies labeling posts from ordinary users on their platforms as inaccurate or misleading, while 45% disapprove.

Again, views vary widely by party. While seven-in-ten Democrats approve of these sites labeling posts from ordinary users as inaccurate or misleading, that share falls to 34% among Republicans. Americans' support—or lack thereof—for flagging content on social media is similar whether applied to posts by politicians or everyday users.

But the public as a whole does not trust that these companies will be able to decide on which posts should be labeled as misleading. Overall, a majority of Americans (66%) say they have not too much or no confidence at all in social media companies being able to determine which posts on their platforms should be labeled as inaccurate or misleading, with 31% saying they have a great deal or some confidence.

Republicans are far more likely than Democrats to express skepticism that social media companies could properly determine which posts should be labeled in this way. More than eight-in-ten Republicans say they have no (50%) or not much (34%) confidence regarding social media companies' ability to determine which posts on their platforms should be labeled.

Democrats are more evenly split in their views: Some 52% of Democrats say they have no confidence at all or not too much confidence in social media companies to determine which posts on their platforms should be labeled as inaccurate or misleading, while 46% say they have a great deal or fair amount of confidence.

CONSERVATIVES BELIEVE THEY ARE CENSORED ONLINE

Claims that conservative voices are being censored online by social media platforms are not backed by evidence and are themselves a disinformation narrative, according to a report released Monday.

The New York University Stern Center for Business and Human Rights' report concluded that anti-conservative bias claims, boosted by some top Republican lawmakers including former President Trump, are not based on any tangible evidence.

"The claim of anti-conservative animus is itself a form of disinformation: a falsehood with no reliable evidence to support it. No trustworthy large-scale studies have determined that conservative content is being removed for ideological reasons or that searches are being manipulated to favor liberal interests," the report stated.

Republicans have ramped up accusations that social media companies have an anti-conservative bias after Facebook and Twitter took action to ban Trump's account following the Jan. 6 riot at the Capitol.

Twitter says it has permanently banned the former president from its platform, while Facebook is leaving the final decision up to its independent oversight body.

Beyond that, there are notable differences along partisan and ideological lines. Six-in-ten conservative Republicans say they have no confidence in social media companies' ability to determine which posts on their platforms should be labeled as misleading, compared with 34% of moderate or liberal Republicans and 11% each of conservative or moderate Democrats and liberal Democrats.

Americans who approve of social media companies labeling posts express more confidence that these sites could properly flag inaccurate content. Indeed, 54% of those who approve of labeling elected officials' posts as misleading say they have at least a fair deal of confidence in social media companies to determine which posts to label, while only 9% of those who disapprove of labeling

The allegation of censorship has been key in Republicans' attacks on Section 230 of the Communications Decency Act, which protects social media platforms from liability associated with third-party content posted on their sites.

Despite the repeated accusations by Republicans, the report found that by "many measures, conservative voices—including that of the ex-president, until he was banished from Twitter and Facebook—often are dominant in online political debates."

For example, the report highlighted the engagement on Trump's Facebook page compared to now-President Biden's page during the three months leading up to Election Day. Trump elicited 87 percent of the total 307 million post interactions between the two, compared to Biden's 13 percent.

Additionally, the report noted that Fox News and Breitbart News led the pack in terms of Facebook interactions with posts by media organizations from Jan. 1 through Nov. 3 of last year. Fox News had 448 million interactions and Breitbart had 295 million; the closest behind them was CNN, at 191 million interactions.

With Biden in office, Republicans have continued to push back against Section 230 over the unfounded accusations of anti-conservative biases.

"Conservative Claims of Online Censorship 'A Form of Disinformation': Study," by Rebecca Clar, The Hill, February 1, 2021.

elected officials' posts say the same. A similar pattern is present when asked about this type of labeling for ordinary users.

The confidence gap between Republicans and Democrats remains present even among those who approve of this type of flagging. Some 56% of Democrats who approve of social media platforms labeling elected officials' posts as inaccurate say they have at least a fair amount of confidence in these companies to determine which posts to label, compared with 42% of Republicans who approve of labeling elected officials' posts as misleading or inaccurate. This partisan gap is even larger among those who approve of labeling ordinary users' posts. Roughly six-in-ten Democrats (58%) who approve of labeling ordinary users' posts express a great deal or a fair amount of confidence in social media companies to determine which posts to label, while 30% of their Republican counterparts say that.

Majorities across parties—but particularly Republicans—say it is at least somewhat likely social media sites censor political views they find objectionable

Americans by and large believe social media companies are censoring political viewpoints they find objectionable. Roughly three-quarters of Americans (73%) think it is very or somewhat likely that social media sites intentionally censor political viewpoints they find objectionable, including 37% who say this is very likely.

Larger shares in both parties think it's likely that these sites engage in political censorship, but this belief is especially widespread among Republicans. Fully 90% of Republicans say that social media sites intentionally censor political viewpoints that they find objectionable—with 60% saying this is very likely the case. By comparison, fewer Democrats believe this to be very (19%) or somewhat (40%) likely.

Republicans—but not Democrats—are divided along ideological lines on the issue. Conservative Republicans are far more likely than moderate or liberal Republicans to say it is very likely that social media sites intentionally censor political viewpoints they find objectionable (70% vs. 44%). Similar shares of moderate or conservative Democrats (20%) and liberal Democrats (18%) express this view.

While these overall views about censorship are on par with those in 2018, there has been a slight uptick in the share of Republicans who think censorship is likely the norm on social media. Today, 90% of Republicans believe it is very or somewhat likely that social media sites intentionally censor political viewpoints—a modest yet statistically significant increase from 2018, when 85% expressed this view. The share of conservative Republicans who say this is very likely the case rose 7 points, from 63% in 2018 to 70% in 2020. Views among moderate and liberal Republicans, as well as Democrats across the ideological spectrum, have not significantly changed since 2018.

Roughly seven-in-ten Republicans say major technology companies tend to support the views of liberals over conservatives

While most Republicans and Democrats believe it's likely that social media sites engage in censoring political viewpoints, they do diverge on which views they think major technology companies tend to favor.

On a broad level, a plurality of Americans say major technology companies tend to support the views of liberals over conservatives, rather than conservatives over liberals (43% vs. 13%). Still, about four-in-ten (39%) say major tech companies tend to support the views of conservatives and liberals equally. The share who say major technology companies equally support the views of conservatives and liberals has slightly decreased since 2018, while the other two sentiments are statistically unchanged.

Public attitudes on this issue are highly partisan. Today, 69% of Republicans say major technology companies favor the views of liberals over conservatives, while 22% say these companies support the views of liberals and conservatives equally. Few Republicans (5%) believe that conservative sentiments are valued more than liberal ones by these companies.

By comparison, one-quarter of Democrats say major technology companies support liberal views over conservative ones, while 19% say conservative sentiments are the ones that are more valued. About half of Democrats (52%) believe tech companies treat these views equally.

There are also large differences when accounting for political ideology. For example, 81% of conservative Republicans say big technology companies favor liberal views, compared with half of moderate or liberal Republicans and even smaller shares of conservative or moderate Democrats (24%) and liberal Democrats (26%).

When asked about the preference of conservative views, 23% of liberal Democrats—a slightly larger share than the 16% in 2018— say that major technology companies favor these views over liberal ones, compared with 10% or fewer of moderate to liberal and conservative Republicans.

"The fear that a privately-owned company succumbs to private interests when censoring content is certainly not far-fetched."

Regulating Social Media Is a Daunting Task

Ingmar Schumacher

In the following viewpoint, Ingmar Schumacher argues that social media is in need of some form of regulation. Though Schumacher supports freedom of speech, he notes that such liberty stops when it harms others or infringes on the rights of others. Imposing regulations on social media is no easy task. Trusting technology companies to self-regulate is a dicey proposition, especially if the companies have their own social or political agenda. But until governments can create a better system, companies have the responsibility to police themselves. Ingmar Schumacher is professor of environmental economics at IPAG Business School in Paris, France.

As you read, consider the following questions:

1. How did German chancellor Angela Merkel offer a rare show of support for Donald Trump?
2. How does the author distinguish between misinformation, disinformation, and malinformation?
3. What solutions does he suggest for regulating the internet?

"Should Social Media Platforms Be Allowed to Censor?" by Ingmar Schumacher, January 18, 2021. Reprinted by permission.

Social media outlets such as Twitter and Facebook are nowadays among the major platforms that are able to quickly disseminate news to a large audience. For example, Facebook counts 2.5 billion users, and a message sent at one end of the world immediately reaches the other end. Politicians such as Donald Trump have understood that their messages spread much faster through social media than traditional news outlets. In fact, Donald Trump has used Twitter as a main means of communication. However, he has recently been banned from various social media platforms because he forwarded false claims about the election and, in addition, wrote tweets that, in Twitter's words, "are in violation of [its] Glorification of Violence Policy." This is the first time that a politician holding such a renowned office as the Presidency of the United States of America has been banned from social media and the reason for which the debate of censorship on social media platforms has arisen.

Some do not agree that social media platforms have the right to ban anyone. Germany's chancellor Angela Merkel, in a rare move that seemingly aids Donald Trump, argued that social media is not allowed to censor, as freedom of speech is a fundamental right. Others would, in addition, argue that social media platforms are now extremely powerful and if they can censor someone such as Donald Trump then they may hold the key to future elections and can direct the information and news that anyone on this planet reads. This is a power that, until not long ago, was only in the hands of national governments, while nowadays it is in the hands of a very few privately owned companies. The question is whether these privately owned companies are following some agenda and thus direct the news, or whether they are simply silent observers that only intervene if their policies are violated.

Given the fact that the major social media platforms have such a depth of reach it is clear that they have, to a large degree, overtaken the existing news broadcasting of the traditional news channels and are the main sources of information of many people. It is thus important to figure out whether these platforms should have the right to censor, or, if they should not have the right to censor, then who should be allowed to undertake this task. In line with this problem goes the question as to how one should deal with the spreading of false news during the era of the internet, where any kind of tweet can be immediately spread even into remote corners of the world and thus have a strongly cascading effect. There are several points at stake, which are freedom of speech, as well as responsibility of content.

While freedom of speech is a fundamental right, this right stops where the speech starts to harm someone else. As John Steward Mill wrote, "power can be rightfully exercised over any member of a civilized community, against his will, [in order] to prevent harm to others." There is currently no internationally accepted regulation that makes social media platforms accountable for its content, and only the person who placed the harmful content online can be held responsible.

Making someone responsible is far from easy, as the lines between misinformation, malinformation and disinformation are fuzzy, to say the least. Misinformation is spreading false information, independent of any intent. Disinformation, in contrast, is spreading misinformation with intent. Malinformation is spreading true information but with the intent of harm. As one can see, it may not be a simple task to classify information into the one or the other category, though the researchers Baines and Elliott have recently tried. Proving the intent of achieving a certain objective by spreading information is an even more complicated process.

For this reason there is a trend towards pushing responsibility, and thus accountability, onto the platforms that allow the harmful content to be placed online. Some countries such as Germany or France have already placed at least some responsibility on social media platforms themselves and ask these to remove hate speech or disinformation. While the European Union is moving towards placing responsibility on the social media platforms themselves, this has not been the case for the USA.

Until a clear regulation of responsibility and accountability is levied on the internet, social media platforms, in theory, have the right to include whatever content they like. Most social media platforms, however, do not simply want to publish just everything. When users sign up to a platform, then these users are asked to acknowledge certain rules and regulations. A user who does not adhere to a platform's rules must then face the consequences that the platform laid out in its terms of use. Some platforms differ in their approach. Platforms such as Twitter have clearly set rules and policies that a user must adhere to, while Parler allows about every opinion to be voiced freely. As Donald Trump did not adhere to the terms of use of various social media platforms, then it is in the right of these platforms to ban him from using these any further. If there is a proclaimed public interest that someone like Donald Trump should be allowed to give his opinion, then this in turn should be done via the official, governmentally-owned channels.

As noted above, since social media platforms have a much faster and deeper reach nowadays than even official government channels, some argument can be made to support the view that the ability to censor should not rest with a privately-owned company that may eventually use its power to direct opinion. This leads to the question of who watches the watchdog. Imagine that Donald Trump had owned Twitter, then he would certainly not have been banned but he might have instead banned other users that speak up against him. The fear that a privately-owned company succumbs to private interests when censoring content is certainly not far-fetched.

Thus, the responsibility and ability to censor should rest with a neutral, benevolent and independent body. Assuming generally acceptable rules and regulations can be laid out and assuming that an oversight institution of this kind can be put in place, then it seems clear it is preferable that censorship is undertaken by this institution than by a privately-owned company. However, until an internationally acceptable oversight institution is put in place, someone has to regulate the social media. It makes sense then that regulation is undertaken by the platforms themselves who allow the content to be uploaded onto their servers. Just as newspapers or radio stations are responsible for the content that they print, social media platforms need to be responsible for the content that they help disseminate.

The bottom line is that the internet needs regulation that is able to blend modern social media with the kind of information that used to be provided by journalists that were adhering to the journalists' creed. Given the vast amount of information that is disseminated by social media every day, this is certainly a daunting yet necessary task.

Periodical and Internet Sources Bibliography

The following articles have been selected to supplement the diverse views presented in this chapter.

Clyde Wayne Crews, Jr. "We're Not Biased, We're Liberals: How Cultural Leftism Will Slant Social Media Regulation," *Forbes*, February 17, 2020, https://www.forbes.com/sites/waynecrews /2020/02/17/were-not-biased-were-liberals-how-cultural -leftism-will-slant-social-media-regulation/.

Editorial Board, "Facebook Needs to Empower Parents, Not Censor Political Speech," *Wall Street Journal*, October 5, 2021, https:// www.wsj.com/articles/facebook-in-the-dock-congress-frances -haugen-mark-zuckerberg-11633471560.

Vera Eidelman, "The Problem with Censoring Political Speech Online—Including Trump's," ACLU, June 15, 2021, https://www .aclu.org/news/free-speech/the-problem-with-censoring -political-speech-online-including-trumps/.

Glenn Greenwald, "Facebook and Twitter Cross a Line Far More Dangerous Than What They Censor," *The Intercept*, October 15, 2020, https://theintercept.com/2020/10/15/facebook-and-twitter -cross-a-line-far-more-dangerous-than-what-they-censor/.

Jameel Jaffer and Katie Fallow, "Official Censorship Should Have No Place in the Digital Public Square," *New York Times*, April 7, 2021, https://www.nytimes.com/2021/04/07/opinion/trump -twitter-first-amendment.html.

Molly Roberts, "Opinion: We Can't Pretend the New Social Media Normal Doesn't Come with Costs of Its Own," *Washington Post*, June 9, 2021, https://www.washingtonpost.com /opinions/2021/06/09/safety-is-starting-outrun-free-speech -online-are-we-okay-with-that/.

Jillian York, "Opinion: Facebook Thought It Was Solving a Problem. It Just Got Handed a Bigger One," Politico, May 7, 2021, https:// www.politico.com/news/magazine/2021/05/07/facebook -oversight-board-trump-ban-social-media-censorship-485608.

OPPOSING
VIEWPOINTS®
SERIES

CHAPTER 4

Should There Be Censorship in Academics?

Chapter Preface

Colleges and universities, with some exceptions, are liberal enclaves. Studies show that a large percentage of professors lean left. Students, as well, being young and often socially open-minded, tend to skew liberal. Again, there are exceptions. Business departments, for one, often have more fiscally conservative members. Schools with religious affiliations, such as Liberty University and Brigham Young University, usually have more conservative faculty and students.

But overall, universities and colleges are little islands of liberalism. It is not unheard of to hear calculus teaching assistants spew Marxist asides in the middle of lectures or for women's studies professors to take it for granted that everyone should know the latest gender pronouns. College professors work together; they socialize among themselves. Liberalism breeds more liberalism.

It is not a given that such professors "indoctrinate" their students with their own political ideology. Students are encouraged to think for themselves and entertain a wide range of social and political ideas. But it certainly may be true that on college campuses, avowing certain concepts that include bias or prejudice, for example, simply won't float. Other students, if not professors, will call out hate speech, or biased statements, or closed-mindedness. That is a given on campus.

Such actions have likely led to self-censorship, where students suppress their opinions for fear that they will be met with derision. But this is not entirely a new phenomenon. People in general know their audience and have always—if they are socially savvy and want to keep their friends and make new ones—weighed their words before speaking. Ill-chosen words have led to the demise of many a friendship long before the new censorship came into being. This self-censorship seems to be most common among conservative students on liberal campuses—yet it is more than likely that the same phenomenon occurs among progressive students at conservative colleges.

Even though college students and faculties skew liberal on most US campuses, there is another element at play when it comes to university politics. At a surface level, campus rules are set by faculty and administration, which skew liberal. But colleges and universities are run by school presidents and their advisory council—commonly known as the board of trustees. Private college trustees are most commonly elected by alumni; public university trustees are selected by state legislatures and governors. These trustees are often successful, wealthy business types, lawyers, or other professionals with strong ties to the college. And they tend to be far more conservative than the students and faculty of colleges they represent.

A study of political contributions at highly regarded Emory University in Georgia, for example, found that over 98% of trustee political donations to Senate candidates in 2020 went to Republicans. Emory employees, according to the same study, overwhelmingly favored Democrats.

In North Carolina, the trustees of North Carolina at Chapel Hill's (UNC) board, for example, are majority Republican, because they are appointed by the Republican-dominated state legislature. In 2021, these trustees initially denied tenure to Nikole Hannah-Jones, the Pulitzer Prize–winning Black journalist who led the *New York Times'* 1619 Project, which examined the history of slavery in America. The 1619 Project has been heavily criticized in the right-wing media. That the trustees later changed their mind and offered her tenure did not help matters. She declined the position at UNC and took one at Howard University instead. Hannah-Jones was essentially canceled at UNC, which indicates that campus cancel culture is not entirely a liberal phenomenon.

> *"If angry majorities have the right to silence speakers by impeding events and shouting speakers down, we wouldn't have had the abolitionist or civil rights movements."*

Banning Controversial Speakers Is Counter to the Aims of Higher Education

Phil Ciciora

In the following viewpoint, Phil Ciciora interviews Vikram Amar, dean of the University of Illinois College of Law, about the complexities inherent in dealing with controversial and hate speech on campus. Though Amar does not believe that all controversial speakers are worth inviting to campus or listening to, he still argues that even hateful speakers should not be banned. It is up to those who disagree with controversial speakers to counter their arguments with more reasonable and rational discourse. Ideas should be evaluated on their substance and rejected when appropriate. The way to counter unacceptable speech is through counter ideas. Phil Ciciora is the business and law editor for the Illinois News Bureau.

"How Should Universities Handle Controversial Speech?" by Phil Ciciora, Business and Law editor, University of Illinois Urbana-Champaign News Bureau, August 30, 2017. Reprinted by permission.

As you read, consider the following questions:

1. Why does Amar feel that not all controversial speakers are worth listening to?
2. Why, according to Amar, is most controversial speech uttered in a public setting protected by freedom of speech?
3. How does Amar distinguish between academic freedom and free speech?

Vikram Amar is the dean of the University of Illinois College of Law and the Iwan Foundation Professor of Law. Amar, an expert in constitutional law, spoke with News Bureau business and law editor Phil Ciciora about the intersection of free speech and academic freedom.

In response to the violence at the University of Virginia, Charlottesville, do you foresee colleges and universities inviting fewer speakers who could be deemed controversial, simply in order to avoid protests or stoking ire?

I hope universities don't overreact by avoiding controversial speakers altogether. Universities must remain committed to promoting and protecting a wide-ranging and open exchange of competing ideas, hypotheses, perspectives and values, and such an exchange often will unavoidably involve political controversy. So if you eliminate controversy, you lose important speech.

At the same time, just because a speaker is controversial doesn't mean that person is worth inviting and listening to. Many of the controversial speakers whom student organizations seek to bring to campuses these days are mere rabble-rousers who do not contribute anything meaningful to the kind of serious discourse that universities should be in the business of facilitating. Central campus administrations, especially at public colleges, may not be easily able to control the choices student and faculty groups make about whom to invite, but the inviters themselves often need to think harder before concluding that someone is really worth hearing.

What is the line between transgressive speech and hate speech?
There is no accepted legal definition of hate speech. For that reason, even though the term is used a lot, it is of limited utility. Much speech that is fully protected by the First Amendment is extremely hateful; just look at the political campaigns we endured last fall. So government, including public universities as well as private schools that adopt constitutional norms, cannot punish speech simply on the ground that the speech is mean-spirited or disparaging. Instead, government can—and should—prohibit and punish true threats, pervasive harassment of individuals,

COMEDIANS AREN'T ALLOWED TO BE FUNNY ON COLLEGE CAMPUSES

The current state of college campuses is no laughing matter—literally.

In a recent Vice News report aired on HBO, bookers for campus comedy tours admitted something that the general public—and comedians themselves—have known for a long time: Comedians aren't allowed to be funny on college campuses.

These bookers explain that before booking a comedian, they request that he or she omit any jokes from their routine that might offend a variety of protected classes: sexual assault survivors, transgender persons, etc. One of these bookers quips, "I can talk about my experience, but I can't make fun of someone else's identity."

The Vice News report offers two opposing takes on the situation.

The first theory is that college students are simply entitled and delusional. In the interview, comedienne Judy Gold, who, like Jerry Seinfeld, refuses to play college campuses, claims young people simply can't take a joke. She attributes their humorlessness to their nonsensical belief that words are more dangerous than actions. College students demand the world adjust to them when, in fact, they should be adjusting to the world, Gold claims.

incitement to violence, etc., all of which are legal categories of expression that fall outside of First Amendment protection.

What constitutes a true threat or actionable harassment often depends much on context. But, in general, things uttered in public—at a speech or rally, or on a sign displayed on a street corner or quad, for example—that do not target specific individuals or call for imminent lawless action are more likely to be fully constitutionally protected and thus immune from government punishment on the basis of the message.

Two other points: First, although hateful speech cannot be prohibited, universities can, and ought to, educate students and faculty about its costs, and can encourage individuals to exercise expressive rights responsibly and with an eye toward the harm inflicted on others. Second, administrators of universities—even

The second theory is that these campus crybabies are a small minority of college students who miss the whole point of comedy itself. The Vice interviewer, Michael Moynihan, correctly points out the flawed logic of the "P.C. Police": College students can't be more diverse than ever, yet all have the same monolithic opinion as to what is and isn't funny. He also asks whether or not the whole point of comedy is to trigger people, and whether or not comedians are supposed to work out their own personal trauma on stage through humor.

To these sane and salient points, the bookers answer in the negative and ironically claim that comedians who refuse to stop being offensive will simply not be booked. In short, they defend their censorship by appealing to the free market, something which leftists usually denounce—unless it serves their purposes.

But make no mistake, this is not about the free market catering to the majority of students' preferences, nor is it about protecting students from "retraumatization." It is about stomping out any kind of fun and creating a reign of terror on campus. As George Orwell said, "every joke is a revolution," and the best means of ensuring the continued rule of the P.C. Police is by policing humor itself.

"Comedians Aren't Allowed to Be Funny on College Campuses," by Troy Worden, *Washington Examiner*, May 31, 2018.

public universities—can themselves speak up, and call out hateful (though fully constitutionally protected) speech for what it is.

What is the proper way for individuals to register dissent with speech that they disagree with? When does protesting someone else's speech veer into preventing speech, and why is that problematic?

Our system is premised on the notion that the answer to bad speech is more speech, so demonstrations and counter-rallies and protests are to be allowed, even encouraged. But the purpose has to be to present the opposing view, not to prevent the original speaker from being heard. So blockades, shouting down speakers, and violence or threatened violence against a speaker or a speaker's audience are all out of bounds. These tactics are in tension with, rather than in furtherance of, the free speech tradition of the First Amendment, which is grounded on the notion that ideas, rather than the use of force, should move hearts and minds.

If angry majorities have the right to silence speakers by impeding events and shouting speakers down, we wouldn't have had the abolitionist or civil rights movements.

In higher education, how are the principles of freedom of speech and academic freedom interconnected? Is one more limited than the other?

That's a hard question because, like hate speech, academic freedom means different things to different people.

In general terms, freedom of speech is a right codified in the federal First Amendment and state constitutional analogues that protects speakers in both public and private settings from unwarranted government interference with expression, to facilitate democracy and preserve autonomy. Academic freedom, by contrast, is grounded on the specific idea that, at least in the academy, free inquiry unburdened by the constraints of orthodoxy will lead to the development of new ideas and knowledge.

Academic freedom is narrower than freedom of speech in that the former applies only on campuses, but it also may in some ways be broader. For example, under the First Amendment, a public university, in its role as employer, may be permitted to direct the specific content of the research or teaching of its faculty, but academic freedom norms suggest that neither the state legislature nor the university administration should micromanage research and teaching directions of individual faculty members once these individuals have been hired, especially after they have been given tenure.

Notwithstanding their different scopes, both freedom of speech and academic freedom rest on the bedrock belief that ideas and arguments ought to be evaluated on their substance. The essence of both kinds of freedom is the opportunity to persuade others of the merits of one's argument, rather than to use power to coerce others into acceding to the proponent's point of view.

> *"To the extent that [it] forcibly subordinates the interests of society to one group's subjective interest, No-Platforming is fundamentally at odds with social justice."*

Only the Very Worst Speakers Should Be Banned on Campus

Monica Richter

In the following viewpoint, Monica Richter raises the issue of "no-platforming" in the United Kingdom, where those who are found offensive are denied a platform to speak. The justification for this censorship is that those who are offensive might cause emotional, psychological, or social damage to listeners. However, Richter argues that the basis for censoring speakers is highly subjective, and that without objective measures in place by which to judge the level of harm to audience members, the intellectual foundations of no-platforming are shaky. Monica Richter is a postgraduate student in European politics and society at St. Antony's College, University of Oxford.

"Only the Most Noxious of Speakers Should Be Banned on Campus," by Monica Richter, Aeon Media Group, January 14, 2016. https://aeon.co/ideas/is-it-legitimate-to-ban-speakers-from-college-campuses. This article was originally published on Aeon (aeon.co) and has been republished under a Creative Commons license.

As you read, consider the following questions:

1. Which prominent personalities have been no-platformed, according to the viewpoint?
2. What does law professor Eugene Volokh mean by "censorship envy"?
3. How is the controversy over British writer Julie Bindel relevant to Richter's argument?

Activists at universities and beyond are increasingly using so-called "No-Platform" arguments to ban the public speech of those whose views they find offensive. In practice, this typically involves staging protests or petitioning university authorities to disinvite "offensive" individuals from speaking engagements. Examples abound from both sides of the Atlantic: in the United States, students have No-Platformed the likes of Condoleezza Rice, Ayaan Hirsi Ali and Christine Lagarde, while in the United Kingdom their targets have included Maryam Namazie and Germaine Greer, among others.

At times, No-Platforming is also used to silence speech about certain topics, as with the cancelled student debate on abortion at Oxford. In all these cases from the past year or so, the justification for No-Platforming is more or less the same: that allowing the person in question to speak would cause some kind of "harm"—not physical harm, but psychological, emotional or social damage—to an individual, group, or even society at large. Indeed, No-Platforming is primarily a tool of identity politics activists who seek to protect minority groups that feel threatened or marginalised by the existing social order. In essence, then, the goal of No-Platforming is greater social justice, realised through the equalisation of power relations. The means to this end is pre-emptive censorship of speech in certain contexts.

Those who challenge No-Platforming are often interpreted uncharitably by its advocates, and are accused of failing to acknowledge the real harm or offence that speech can cause, particularly to marginalised groups. Let me make, therefore, a disclaimer that I hope deflects this move. I am not advocating an "anything goes" approach to free speech. This is an untenable position, as the rightful bans on child pornography, perjury, extortion and much else illustrate. I acknowledge that speech can cause real harm, and that it should be limited in those rare cases in which it does. I even agree that No-Platforming might sometimes be an appropriate means of pre-empting such harm, for example in cases of probable incitement to violence or psychological trauma. However, I wish to raise questions about the nature of the harm that can legitimately justify restrictions on speech, and the way in which it is discovered.

Contemporary advocates of No-Platforming have so far failed to provide any convincing, rigorous definition of "harm" to justify their practice. Typically, they claim that offensive speech undermines the "personhood" of those it targets. However, in the vast majority of cases, they fail to demonstrate how this alleged violation occurs, nor even what they mean by "personhood." The intellectual foundations of No-Platforming are thus very shaky. There are two reasons for this. First, justifications for No-Platforming fail to separate cases of genuine harm from those of trivial offence or discomfort. Second, in failing to make that distinction, No-Platforming hinders the progress of social justice.

When the No-Platform principle emerged in the 1970s, it was explicitly restricted to racist or fascist speech, with "harm" clearly defined as incitement to racial hatred or to violence. The problem with today's No-Platform movement is a lack of precision about what is meant by "harm." Instead, No-Platformers tender a wide range of reasons for their practice, including feeling uncomfortable, threatened, unsafe or offended. These complaints do not constitute harm in the same tangible or objective way as, for instance, incitement to violence. Rather, they are claims of purely subjective experience.

This premise is central to the contemporary politics of identity. Subjective experience, the argument goes, is by definition exclusive: it is unknowable to those who do not have the relevant identity characteristic. The subjective experience of womanhood, for example, is unknowable to any man; that of being black is unknowable to anyone white; that of being transgender is unknowable to anyone cis. Accordingly, the subjective harm claimed by a particular identity group cannot be questioned by any other. To put it differently, if one member feels harmed by some speech, then they have been harmed ipso facto. By this logic, all claims of subjective experience must be considered equally valid.

It is easy to see how readily this position becomes exploitable. If No-Platforming can be justified exclusively on the basis of a given group's subjective experience, we cannot ensure that petty cases—based on minor discomfort or even mere disagreement with some speech, yet cloaked in the language of offence or harm—are dismissed. In other words, we have no way of adjudicating between requests for No-Platform when we lack an objective measure for determining which requests ought to be upheld, and which ought not.

To understand the practical consequences of this problem, it is useful to consider the phenomenon that Eugene Volokh, law professor at the University of California, Los Angeles, calls "censorship envy." An initial request by a given identity group to censor some speech on the basis of claimed harm prompts analogous requests from other identity groups. No-Platforming becomes contagious. Consistency requires that once we allow some speech bans due to claimed harm, we cannot justifiably deny other requests made on the same grounds, since, given the unknowability of others' subjective experience, all claims of harm must be treated as equal. And inevitably, at some point, these claims come into conflict.

The ongoing controversy surrounding the British writer Julie Bindel, for instance, exemplifies this problem. Bindel is a trans-exclusionary feminist, and has been No-Platformed by the UK's National Union of Students on grounds of alleged transphobia. But how can this decision be reconciled with the equally valid claim of trans-exclusionary feminists that womanhood is contingent upon being biologically female? These feminists can likewise, legitimately, request to No-Platform trans-inclusive viewpoints. The upshot is that no one at all gets to speak about the issue. This leaves us at a stalemate: the logical consequence is emphatic silence on nearly every issue that bears upon identity.

In a pluralistic society, justice requires that we balance the competing interests of different groups in the fairest way possible. We need to be able to communicate what we believe, so that we can persuade others that our interests should be acted upon collectively. To the extent that No-Platforming forcibly subordinates the interests of society to one group's subjective interest, without providing any way to determine whether that subordination is in fact just, No-Platforming is fundamentally at odds with social justice. Its claim to be a moral form of censorship is baseless and a smokescreen. To be legitimate, any No-Platform principle should be founded upon a consensual and objective understanding of the kind of harm that justifies curtailment of speech. Wide-ranging freedom of expression is too important both to education and to democracy to be restricted in the name of an activism based on subjective perceptions of harm.

VIEWPOINT 3

> *"Free speech is easy when thoughtful speakers we agree with are being silenced. The real test is when idiots we hate try to speak, and the protests against them cost a lot of money."*

Banning Speakers on Campus Is Wrong
John K. Wilson

In the following viewpoint, John K. Wilson defends the right to free speech, even for those whom he classifies as "idiots." The author disagrees with the University of California, Berkeley's then-new policy of rejecting controversial speakers because their appearance might lead to security issues and also might cost exorbitant amounts for security. Rioting has become a form of censorship, Wilson argues, that is antithetical to the principles that colleges were built on. John K. Wilson is the author of The Myth of Political Correctness: The Conservative Attack on Higher Education *and* How the Left Can Win Arguments and Influence People: A Tactical Manual for Pragmatic Progressives.

As you read, consider the following questions:

1. Why does Wilson reject the notion that speakers can be rejected for potential incitement to violence?
2. What is the "heckler's veto" that Wilson refers to?
3. How is the AAUP's statement on freedom of speech on campus at odds with Berkeley's policy?

"Why Banning Speakers Is Absolutely Wrong," by John K. Wilson, Academe Blog, September 26, 2017. Reprinted by permission.

Milo Yiannopoulos' much-hyped Free Speech Week at Berkeley has disappeared, not with a bang but with a whimper. The whimper came yesterday when Milo made a brief appearance on Sproul Plaza, where he sang the Star-Spangled Banner (without kneeling) and left about 30 minutes later. Berkeley spent an estimated $800,000 on security for the event. Several dozen supporters showed up to hear Milo, and a few hundred protesters.

Milo has made himself the poster child for free speech on campus, and because people hate Milo, they've begun to question campus free speech, too. But banning speakers is wrong, even when it's done for financial reasons, and even when it takes the form of imposing security costs on those who invite controversial speakers. Berkeley is creating a financial version of the heckler's veto, and it must be rejected.

Why did Free Speech Week get cancelled? It's easy to blame Milo, because he represents the combination of vile beliefs repulsively expressed and gross incompetence in arranging an event. Free Speech Week was plagued by missed deadlines and fake news, with various announcements of speakers who had not agreed to speak (and in some cases had never been asked).

But there is a bigger issue here about the principle of free speech on campus. I believe in defending that principle, even though Milo is an idiot. And I worry about the policies and practices of the Berkeley administration being enacted to try to stop people like Milo, because the threat to free speech goes far beyond Milo. I'll address Berkeley's flawed policies soon in another post, but here I want to respond to some of the arguments favoring censorship of Milo.

Before Free Speech Week fizzled out, a group of Berkeley faculty demanded that the university ban the event.

The letter declared, "as faculty committed to the safety of our students and our campus, we are calling for a complete boycott of all classes and campus activities while these Alt-Right events are taking place at the very center of UC Berkeley's campus."

The faculty letter was deeply misguided, despite its good intentions. Calling for a campus boycott with the goal of banning certain events and certain speech is an attempt at repression. (However, there is little danger that college administrators ever listen to faculty.)

The letter noted, "In fact, campus safety concerns have already forced the Anthropology Department to cancel a public talk during 'free speech week.' This makes clear that the administration understands the imminent threat to campus safety while also revealing that the loud demands of the Alt-Right has the effect of silencing members of our campus community." The Alt-Right did not silence anyone; overblown fear of protests against the Alt-Right did. There was no good reason why the administration demanded that the Anthropology Department pay extra for security for a planned talk during Free Speech Week (the security at the library would be needed whether there was an event there or not). There was no threat to the talk from the Alt-Right or anyone else.

According to the faculty, "there are forms of speech that are not protected under the First Amendment. These include speech that presents imminent physical danger and speech that disrupts the university's mission to educate. Milo, Coulter and Bannon do not come to educate; they and their followers come to humiliate and incite." This is a false and extremely dangerous narrowing of free speech. Milo's talks presented no imminent physical threat. Incitement to violence is an extremely narrow legal category and one that almost never can be determined in advance of the actual inciting words being spoken. The only danger might have come from left-wing protesters, but the idea that they present a physical threat is really a right-wing smear abetted by the administration's excessive security plans. The notion that a planned speech by a former leading adviser to the president cannot educate someone is wrong. There is a lot to learn from Steve Bannon, albeit mostly by rejecting his terrible ideas. It is extremely dangerous to announce that the government can decide in advance which speeches are educational and which can be banned for the crime of "humiliating" others. I would love to speak at Berkeley about my anti-Trump book, *Trump Unveiled*. But I would certainly try to humiliate Trump and his supporters. Should my talk therefore be banned? Humiliation is not a valid standard.

This letter of faculty declared, "Cancel classes and tell students to stay home. A boycott of classes affirms that our fundamental responsibility as faculty is to protect the safety and well being of all our students. While we understand the argument that canceling classes might be seen as a penalty to students who want to learn—by holding class when some students CAN NOT attend by virtue of their DACA status and the imminent threat that these campus events hold, faculty who DO hold classes are disadvantaging DACA students and others who will feel threatened by being on campus."

But this entire argument for a boycott is based on a false premise. There was no threat to DACA students from allowing Free Speech Week. If right-wing nuts like Milo decide to disclose the status of DACA students, it means literally nothing. The whole point of DACA is that it's a government registry, which means the government already knows who these students are. The idea that students "CAN NOT attend by virtue of their DACA status and the imminent threat" is just absurd. Does anyone think Milo has access to the DACA database? Does anyone imagine ICE agents will suddenly (and illegally) arrest DACA students because Milo identifies them at an event?

If you believe in applying the heckler's veto to Milo and friends, then you open the door to apply it to left-wing speakers, too. The "threat" argument given by these faculty would only justify banning protests against Milo, not Milo himself.

These Berkeley faculty claim: "We refuse to grant the Alt-Right the media spectacle that they so desperately desire." Of course, being banned is exactly the media spectacle that the Alt-Right desire the most. This letter is a gift to the Alt-Right, not an attack on it.

They are not the only ones to draw the worst lessons from Milo. In the *New York Times*, Aaron Hanlon argues, "the reality is that 'free speech on campus' is not resource-neutral." No, it is not. And that's exactly why free speech must be defended according to principles. The cost of security, based on the violence of the opposition, is not a sound principle for silencing free speech.

According to Hanlon, "The question of which campus speakers warrant security funding is real and challenging." Actually, it's not. That's like asking which professors warrant security funding. If a left-wing professor tweets something offensive and receives death threats, should the university fire him with the excuse that he isn't good enough to deserve substantial security funding? Or good enough to deserve the loss of funding from angry donors and politicians? The moment you say that campus freedom should depend on how much it costs the university, you have sacrificed academic freedom and free speech on campus.

Hanlon argues, "When speakers like these cost hundreds of thousands of dollars but add scant academic value, the issue is more complicated than the radical or offensive nature of their views." No, it's not. If you give administrators the power to ban speakers based on the costs imposed on their protesters, it's exactly the same as banning them for having offensive views, except that you're simply outsourcing the logic to security costs.

Every controversial speaker or professor or student on campus has a potential cost, whether it is police or donors or public support or students refusing to attend. Academic freedom demands that universities ignore that cost, and fully protect the freedom of everyone. When it comes to academic appointments, the judgments must be based on academic value; but when it comes to extramural speakers, there are no judgments made by the administration about which speakers are good or bad. It is dangerous to give the administration the power to decide the academic value of speakers when so much money is on the line.

Hanlon calls for "educational standards for who deserves a college platform and financial resources." This is an extremely dangerous stand. There are plenty of speakers on campus—musicians, comedians, and others—who don't serve a clear educational standard and shouldn't. And there are also political provocateurs, left and right, who add to the free exchange of ideas even though they may not meet someone's academic ideal of a speaker. But the biggest problem with Hanlon's theory is that puts an unequal burden on controversial speech. Since controversial speakers are the only ones who require security fees, they will be the only ones banned under Hanlon's proposal. But a university should stand for the value that controversial speech deserves the greatest protection, not the least.

It appears that Berkeley may be embracing Hanlon's approach. Chancellor Christ announced last week that Berkeley would re-examine its policies: "We should explore whether there should be a limit to the number of events a student group can schedule in a row, whether we should have an annual budget for security costs, and whether criteria for status as a student organization should be reviewed."

Let me translate that: Christ wants to ban controversial groups from holding more than a few events, wants to ban them from having events that offend protesters and cost too much in security, and then wants to ban the controversial group entirely if possible. This, needless to say, is a dire threat to free speech. Suppose that a student group draws protests by virtue of their existence. Should they be banned from having weekly meetings? Or merely disbanded when they reach an annual limit in being protested?

Consider this: when Ben Shapiro spoke at Berkeley earlier this month, the College Republicans were required to agree to pay basic security costs of $15,738 in order to reserve a space for him.

In the end, Berkeley says it spent $600,000 protecting Shapiro's speech. Milo was required to pay $65,700 to reserve two indoor spaces on campus, which the administration cancelled anyway.

These are shocking numbers. A typical speaker at Berkeley requires zero security. It is the threat posed to a speaker that leads to security expenses, and charging any student groups for security violates Berkeley's own policies. And yet Berkeley is now planning to find ways to make these groups pay even more money, or face their events being banned.

The high cost of security threatens all controversial speech at Berkeley, especially left-wing speech. Most left-wing and mainstream student groups cannot afford anything close to those figures for a campus speaker. For example, I help organize the Chicago Book Expo, which is being held on Oct. 1 at Columbia College Chicago and features dozens of interesting and controversial speakers. If we had to pay even $2,500 in security fees (more than our entire budget), we would cancel the event forever. Right-wing groups can get Koch money and other billionaires to make some of their events possible. But how many left-wing speakers would be cancelled if groups and departments were charged $15,738 in security fees for each event? 90%? 95%? 99%?

What makes anyone think this won't happen? Do you imagine that white supremacists are such nice people that they would never try to shut down left-wing events by holding protests? Do you imagine that college administrators are fearless fighters against oppression and would never impose security fees to silence offensive left-wing speakers who damage a college's reputation and threaten its fundraising? What exactly is the basis of anyone's hope that the heckler's veto, once institutionalized with security fees, will not blow back against you?

I think the Berkeley Administration wants to escalate its security requirements in order to discourage groups from inviting controversial speakers and in order to justify censoring speakers. Certainly, it makes no sense that a 30-minute peaceful appearance by some nut on a public square should cost a university $800,000 in security costs.

And it has been a highly effective strategy. People who normally would never have considered banning speakers or limiting the number of events a group can organize on campus are suddenly looking at six-figure security costs and deciding that maybe censorship makes financial sense. But that mindset supporting censorship is created by the choices of the administration, the choices of excessive security and control over campus.

So what is the solution to the problem of universities wasting millions of dollars protecting a handful of idiots from the handful of idiots who violently protest them? One solution is that universities shouldn't pay anything for additional security. If Milo decided to speak at a public square in Berkeley, the city of Berkeley police and other government agencies would pay for the security expense of dealing with protesters. The government, not the university, should pay for the cost of policing a protest. And the cost of the police should not be billed to the person or group being protested, any more than a crime victim should be billed for having the police investigate the crime and enforce the law. If a university chooses to take on the role of policing, then it must follow the same rules and cannot bill the person being protested.

The AAUP's 1992 Statement On Freedom of Expression and Campus Speech Codes noted, "On a campus that is free and open, no idea can be banned or forbidden. No viewpoint or message may be deemed so hateful or disturbing that it may not be expressed." The AAUP's 1967 Joint Statement on Rights and Freedoms of Students noted, "Students should be allowed to invite and to hear any person of their own choosing."

These principles do not permit universities to ban "bad" speakers or allow a heckler's veto to prevail, whether by shouting down or violence or its close cousin, the security fee.

Free speech is easy when thoughtful speakers we agree with are being silenced. The real test is when idiots we hate try to speak, and the protests against them cost a lot of money. But it's not a difficult test to pass if you just imagine the positions being reversed. If a speaker you support is being protested by white supremacists, should that speaker be banned because of the expense?

The practice of a university charging groups five-figure fees for controversial speakers is a severe limit on free speech. It is a heckler's fee, and when it reaches thousands and thousands of dollars, it amounts to a veto in most cases. Charging these fees ensures that only controversial speakers with wealthy benefactors (who tend to be conservative) can afford to speak on campus.

Berkeley is sending a clear message to the white supremacists: If you can threaten trouble and damage property like Antifa, then you, too, can effectively censor speakers through security fees. This is how charging for controversial speakers (or banning them) tends to encourage violence rather than preventing it. The only way to stem the violence is to stop rewarding it. For anyone who wants to ban a speaker, rioting has become an effective tool of censorship.

"[Students] may be self-censoring because they feel they will be judged by others on the campus or are considering possible social consequences for what they say, rather than the colleges themselves 'making some speech harder.'"

Self-Censorship Is Common on Campus

Greta Anderson

In the following viewpoint, Greta Anderson argues that while most college students believe that administrators will protect their right to free speech, they still are hesitant to voice controversial ideas on campus. Many students engage in self-censorship out of fear of ridicule, or that an unpopular opinion may affect their grade, or out of hesitance to offend their fellow students or professors. Some students worry that unpopular opinions may hurt their chances at campus jobs or scholarships. Yet colleges are supposed to be bastions for the open exchange of ideas, and these findings, Anderson writes, make it clear that colleges still have a lot of work to do when it comes to free speech. Greta Anderson covers student life and athletics for Inside Higher Ed.

"A Perception Problem About Free Speech," by Greta Anderson, *Inside Higher Ed*, September 29, 2020. Reprinted by permission.

As you read, consider the following questions:

1. What general findings did the FIRE survey reveal about free speech on campus?
2. In what settings were students most comfortable discussing controversial topics?
3. What types of colleges scored poorly when it came to their reputation for defending free speech?

A large survey about free speech and expression on college campuses found that students, especially those in the political minority at an institution, are censoring or editing what they say and are uncomfortable and reluctant to challenge peers and professors on controversial topics.

Sixty percent of students have at one point felt they couldn't express an opinion on campus because they feared how other students, professors or college administrators would respond, according to a survey report published Tuesday by the Foundation for Individual Rights in Education, or FIRE, a campus civil liberties watchdog group, and RealClearEducation, an online news service. The survey of 19,969 undergraduate students from 55 colleges and universities was administered from April to May by College Pulse, a research company.

Sean Stevens, senior research fellow in polling and analytics for FIRE, said the survey is the largest the organization has conducted and possibly the largest survey ever conducted about freedom of speech on campus. Similar recent surveys have had sample sizes of about 3,000 to 5,000 students.

The report digs into whether students feel they can openly engage in specific scenarios, such as when a controversial speaker comes to campus or how comfortable they are speaking about race, abortion or other "controversial" topics in the classroom, Stevens said.

Lara Schwartz, director of American University's Project on Civil Discourse and an expert on campus free speech, said the survey provides a picture of students' perceptions and indicates that students largely see their college as generally supportive of free speech.

When students were asked if college administrators "make it clear to students that free speech is protected" on campus, 70 percent answered yes, the report said. Fifty-seven percent of students also said that if there were a "controversy over offensive speech" on campus, their administrators would be more likely to defend the speaker's First Amendment rights, compared to 41 percent who said that administrators were more likely to punish the speaker in this situation, according to the report.

Schwartz cited these findings as a sign that students generally feel their specific campuses are creating a positive environment for free speech. They may be self-censoring because they feel they will be judged by others on the campus or are considering possible social consequences for what they say, rather than the colleges themselves "making some speech harder," she said.

"Students accurately believe that their schools will protect free expression. That's a good thing," Schwartz said.

Over all, students were more likely to feel comfortable discussing controversial political topics with peers and less comfortable "publicly disagreeing" with a professor about such topics, the report said. One-quarter of students said they felt "very" comfortable discussing the topics with classmates, and 42 percent felt "somewhat" comfortable. One-quarter of students said that they felt "somewhat" uncomfortable with these discussions and 9 percent were "very" uncomfortable.

When asked how they would feel openly disagreeing with their professor, only 15 percent of students said they would be "very" comfortable and 30 percent said "somewhat" comfortable, the report said. Thirty-three percent said they would feel "somewhat" uncomfortable and 22 percent said they were "very" uncomfortable with the idea of disagreeing openly with a professor about a controversial topic.

Robert Shibley, executive director of FIRE, noted that report's goal is to provide prospective students and their parents with a tool to measure the political and cultural climate of individual college campuses and help them gauge whether an institution is friendly to free speech and open debate. FIRE ranked the 55 colleges where responses were collected, including all eight Ivy League institutions, using a zero-to-100 scale that is based on students' survey responses and the colleges' policies for protecting and restricting free speech.

The University of Chicago ranked first over all, and Shibley praised the university's "reputation for defending free speech." The low rankings of large public state institutions, such as the University of Texas at Austin, ranked 54, and Louisiana State University, ranked 53, were "a surprise," he said.

"Obviously where campuses stand on free speech is not going to be as significant to students compared to how much money they have to spend," or *U.S. News & World Report* rankings of the institutions, Shibley said, but it should play a part if students are deciding between different schools, or if students have opinions that are likely to be silenced on a given campus and if they want to engage in activism.

FIRE also developed an average "liberal" and "conservative" score for the colleges based on survey responses from students who are more left- or right-leaning, the report said. Students could use the information to select a college that is more in line with their own ideology or belief, but Shibley said the hope is they evaluate their choices based on how tolerant a specific college would be of all viewpoints.

While the rankings take into account how students with specific ideologies feel about whether their campuses are open to various views, Stevens said an open-ended question at the end of the survey found that many students had personal reasons why they might be self-censoring. Some students are worried that speaking up about controversial topics or sharing an unpopular opinion in class will affect their grade and do not want to offend their professors or classmates, he said. Some also expressed fear of administrative retaliation or mentioned reluctance to criticize their college or university because they are employed by the institution, he said.

Schwartz noted that during her own research for the University of California National Center for Free Speech and Civic Engagement, students also listed dependence on campus jobs and scholarships as a reason to censor or edit their own speech.

Stevens said there were "mirror image comments" from students on opposite sides of the political aisle, who felt uncomfortable speaking up about particular issues because they knew they were in a political minority. Students that identified as Democrats on campuses where they were outnumbered by Republicans felt similarly to students who self-identified as Republicans in an environment with mostly Democratic students, he said.

"One of the most common things that comes up is politics and perceptions," Stevens said. "Whether they're liberal or conservative, if they're in a minority, they're less likely to speak up. That's a pretty prominent theme across the board with the political disagreements."

Stevens said he wasn't surprised to see abortion and race as the top two topics that students found "difficult to have an open and honest conversation about" on their campus. About 44 percent of students surveyed selected these topics; gun control and transgender issues followed close behind, according to the report. Stevens said Black students were more likely to face difficulties having "open and honest" discussions about race than all other ethnic groups.

Sixty-six percent of Black students identified race as a challenging topic versus 43 percent of students over all, the report said. In written responses, students explained that they might be the only Black person in the classroom and it can be uncomfortable to bring up issues of race, or that they are also expected to speak for all Black people during discussions on race, Stevens said.

Schwartz said such problems could come into play when Black students who may have attended predominantly Black high schools enroll at predominantly white institutions. This "culture shock" can also be the same for white students who may experience significantly more diversity on campus than they did in their high schools, and also make it uncomfortable for them to speak about race, she said. Schwartz said these scenarios can also significantly influence how students feel speaking about political issues.

"A lot of the focus that we might give on this self-editing question is much more complex than what's happening on a college campus," Schwartz said. Many students "are coming from homogenous communities and are coming into much more heterogeneous communities in college … People are very unused to being in a community where they're a minority viewpoint."

Schwartz said that the report's findings could be used to illustrate to faculty members and administrators why more work needs to be done educating students to be more tolerant of a range of ideas and on how to effectively have "tough conversations."

There should also be more opportunities for students to learn how to make mistakes and apologize when having controversial discussions, otherwise students see certain speech as being "allowed" or "not allowed," she said.

Shibley said that professors have a responsibility to "set the standard of free inquiry" in the classroom.

"It ought to be a place where people have their beliefs challenged, make different arguments where that's appropriate and understand the strengths and weaknesses on both sides," Shibley said. "That's what makes a meaningful class."

> *"The data suggest that students who felt pressure from conservative faculty members 'frequently' or 'all the time' felt more pressure than did students with liberal professors."*

Colleges Are Not Silencing Conservative Students

Colleen Flaherty

In the following viewpoint, Colleen Flaherty argues that while college professors tend to skew liberal, there is no evidence that they are pressuring conservative students to change their political philosophy. Conservatives have alleged that campuses are breeding grounds for liberal ideology, but this is not proved out in studies. In today's highly charged political atmosphere, conversations about health care, for example, can seem political, which may cause some students to feel uncomfortable, but a recent study suggests that only a small minority of students, 10 percent, reported feeling pressured. The data suggests that it is more often liberal students in classes taught by conservative professors who report feeling pressured. Colleen Flaherty writes about faculty issues for Inside Higher Ed.

"Students, Professors and Politics," by Colleen Flaherty, *Inside Higher Ed*, March 3, 2020. Reprinted by permission.

As you read, consider the following questions:

1. According to the study, how have many students changed their political ideology during college?
2. Why were liberal students in subjects such as business likely to feel pressured?
3. What topics does sociologist Amy Binder consider worth studying regarding politics on campus?

Pundits and lawmakers sometimes accuse professors of being liberals who indoctrinate their students. The research says they are right on one of those points, not both. Faculty members' political beliefs do run left, according to numerous studies. But, counter to what Education Secretary Betsy DeVos and others have alleged, even conservative students don't generally feel pressured to think a certain way.

Preliminary data from a new study suggest that this dynamic might be changing, however—yet not for the reasons one might assume. Ten percent of students in this study, especially conservative ones, did report feeling pressured to align their thinking with their professors' politics. Yet the authors say that this might be because the overall political environment is now so charged, not because professors are telling students what to think.

"There are so many different ways now that students are being cued to think politically, whereas maybe they weren't before," said co-author Matthew Mayhew, the William Ray and Marie Adamson Flesher Professor of Educational Administration at Ohio State University. "If I'm a professor and I'm talking about health care, students in the room might be cued to think politically about it, but 20 years ago that wouldn't necessarily have been the case."

What does this mean for teaching? Mayhew said that professors don't need to change the way they teach, but that they might tell students that "discomfort" with new ideas is part of learning. And that shouldn't be confused with pressure, anxiety or trauma, he said. This, of course, echoes much of the advice academics have shared with students in campus speech debates.

Mayhew further guessed that higher education—generally, and not just whether it should be free—might become one of these automatically "political" topics within the next five years. That's a "scary" prospect, Mayhew said, as higher education is not exclusively part of any one political party's "agenda."

For this part of their study, Mayhew and his colleagues asked 3,486 college seniors from institutions across the U.S. about their observations of faculty members' politics. Forty-nine percent of the sample said that their professors expressed politically liberal views "frequently" or "all the time." Just 9 percent said the same about conservative professors.

As to the indoctrination question, 10 percent of students said they sensed pressure of any kind from professors when it comes to politics. Conservative students were more likely to feel pressure than those who identified as liberal.

Some 47 percent of students reported that they had changed their political leanings during college. Of those, 30 percent said they became more liberal, and 17 percent said they became more conservative. The share of "liberal" students increased 5 percentage points and the share "very liberal" grew by 4 percentage points.

What about students who felt pressure from professors about politics? Of the 10 percent who reported feeling this pressure "frequently" or "all the time," half changed their political leanings by the end of their senior year. And that's just slightly higher than the share of students who changed their political leanings without feeling any, or just occasional, pressure from professors.

Interestingly, the data suggest that students who felt pressure from conservative faculty members "frequently" or "all the time" felt more pressure than did students with liberal professors.

About 30 percent of students say they became more liberal in college, whether or not they felt any pressure from faculty members.

Co-author Alyssa Rockenbach, Alumni Distinguished Graduate Professor of Education at North Carolina State University, said her team's findings "add nuance to and in some ways challenge the narrative that colleges are exclusively liberalizing environments." That is, the data hint at potential shifts in the student experience but also underscore what we already know: that colleges and universities are not indoctrination factories.

While students on the whole tend to perceive liberal perspectives from faculty members more often than conservative perspectives, Rockenbach said, only a "small proportion"—that 10 percent—feel pressured on that front.

Although conservative students feel somewhat more pressure than liberal students, she added, "we don't see evidence that feeling pressured actually results in substantial changes to these students' political inclinations." And when pressure from faculty members does "appear to have an impact, it actually encourages slight conservative shifts among students."

A key piece of the study is that perceived pressure from faculty members depends on academic major. To Mayhew's point on health care—where topics such as universal coverage and abortion might come up—conservative students in nursing, medicine, pharmacy and therapy were more likely to say they felt pressured. That was also true for those in the arts, humanities and religion and for double majors.

Meanwhile, liberal students majoring in the social sciences, education or business were more likely to report feeling pressured. Business, in particular, is known to have more conservative professors than academe over all.

As for the current political climate, Rockenbach said that it "probably" plays a role in students' perceptions of pressure because political conversations in class "may be more salient right now."

So maybe classrooms feel like many other public or semipublic spaces in our political moment. If that's the case, Rockenbach and Mayhew's data offer some hope. Asked if they'd had significant disagreements over political issues with friends during college, 65 percent said no. Twenty-nine percent said they had, but that they remained friends anyway. Just 6 percent said they'd had significant political disagreements and did not remain friends. The study had three check-in points, from 2015 to 2019, when the students were seniors. So these peer-to-peer arguments happened before and after the contentious 2016 election.

Back in the classroom, Rockenbach said that more frequent discussions open up opportunities for students to feel pressure from certain professors, "particularly if the students' own views are on the other end of the political spectrum." So are such conversations a no-go? Rockenbach's answer: "I don't think so. These exchanges have strong potential to enhance student learning, help them refine their own beliefs and values, and empower their political engagement."

At the same time, Rockenbach cautioned that it's "critical for faculty to create classroom spaces that encourage authenticity and respectful dialogue." When and if professors decide to share their own perspectives, she added, it's "important that they simultaneously encourage students' freedom to disagree and offer different viewpoints."

The group's findings were published for the first time as an op-ed in the *Washington Post*. Rockenbach and Mayhew led the study with the Interfaith Youth Core group. The data, drawn from their Interfaith Diversity Experiences and Attitudes Longitudinal Survey, also contain insights about students' perceptions on LGBT issues, spirituality and religion, but those figures aren't quite ready for prime time.

Amy Binder, professor of sociology at the University of California, San Diego, co-wrote a book on college students' political experiences in 2012 and is working on another one. Of the new study, Binder said the "devil is in the details," in that she'd like to know more about what kind of pressure students sense. "Do they feel pressure to write their exams in a particular way to get a good grade? To speak up in class parroting a professor's perceived ideology?" she asked. "To become liberal or conservative because they are majoring in a particular discipline? To attend, or not attend, rallies or protests?"

Binder further noted that "influencing" an opinion is different than pressuring someone to change theirs. She guessed that numbers might be at play, at least in the finding that conservative professors influence their students more. Maybe if there are more liberal students taking business courses than there are conservative students taking humanities courses in the sample, she wondered, "you can see a pattern where conservative faculty are more persuasive in sheer numbers."

Mayhew said that more students identifed as liberal than conservative, and students appreciated politically liberal ideologies to a greater degree than conservative ones across three time points. But he said that the finding about conservative professors might be more about students' expectations. College is seen as "liberalizing," he said, so students "might be surprised and possibly intimidated by the mere expression of their professors' conservative ideologies." Reiterating his point about discomfort, he said that feeling often arises "when expectations misalign with experience."

Periodical and Internet Sources Bibliography

The following articles have been selected to supplement the diverse views presented in this chapter.

Jeremy Bauer-Wolf, "Reclaiming Their Campuses," *Inside Higher Ed*, March 21, 2018, https://www.insidehighered.com /news/2018/03/21/colleges-changing-their-policies-after-visits -controversial-speakers.

Conor Friedersdorf, "Evidence That Conservative Students Really Do Self-Censor," *The Atlantic*, February 16, 2020, https://www .theatlantic.com/ideas/archive/2020/02/evidence-conservative -students-really-do-self-censor/606559/.

Evan Gerstmann, "2020: The Year Universities Surrendered Completely to Cancel Culture," *Forbes*, December 28, 2020, https://www.forbes.com/sites/evangerstmann/2021/12/28/2020 -the-year-universities-surrendered-completely-to-cancel -culture/?sh=2a3097d239c7.

Jacob Hess, "The Courage to Not Cancel," *Deseret News*, August 8, 2021, https://www.deseret.com/opinion/2021/8/8/22568732 /cancel-culture-at-universities-higher-education-courage-utah -valley-university.

Jeffrey Adam Sachs, "Do Universities Have a Self-Censorship Problem?" *The Washington Post*, April 16, 2019, https://www .washingtonpost.com/politics/2019/04/16/do-universities-have -self-censorship-problem/.

Jennifer Schubert-Akin, "The Consequences of Campus Cancel Culture," *Washington Examiner*, March 27, 2021, https://www .washingtonexaminer.com/opinion/the-consequences-of -campus-cancel-culture.

Asheesh Kapur Siddique, "Campus Cancel Culture Freakouts Obscure the Power of University Boards," *Teen Vogue*, May 19, 2021, https://www.teenvogue.com/story/campus-cancel-culture -university-boards.

Rafael Walker, "How Canceling Controversial Speakers Hurts Students," *Chronicle of Higher Education*, February 8, 2017, https://www.chronicle.com/article/how-canceling-controversial -speakers-hurts-students/.

For Further Discussion

Chapter 1

1. After reading the viewpoints in this chapter, what is your opinion on cancel culture?
2. Do you believe cancel culture is a problem in society?
3. What criteria, if any, do you believe should lead to a person being canceled?

Chapter 2

1. After reading the viewpoints in this chapter, do you believe that critical race theory and the 1619 Project should be taught in K–12 schools?
2. Does teaching about America's racial past divide the country?
3. Is it still necessary to confront America's racist past or should this conversation be retired?

Chapter 3

1. After reading these viewpoints, do you believe that social media has become too powerful?
2. Should the government be allowed to censor hate speech on social media?
3. Should social media companies be more aggressive in censoring inappropriate material?

Chapter 4

1. After reading the viewpoints in this chapter, what is your opinion on allowing controversial speakers to give talks on campus?
2. Is self-censorship a problem on college campuses?
3. Should students be able to prevent speakers they object to from appearing on campus?

Organizations to Contact

The editors have compiled the following list of organizations concerned with the issues debated in this book. The descriptions are derived from materials provided by the organizations. All have publications or information available for interested readers. The list was compiled on the date of publication of the present volume; the information provided here may change. Be aware that many organizations take several weeks or longer to respond to inquiries, so allow as much time as possible.

American Association of University Professors (AAUP)

1133 Nineteenth Street NW, Suite 200
Washington, DC 20036
(201) 737-5900
email: aaup@aaup.org
website: www.aaup.org

The AAUP helps to shape American higher education by developing the standards and procedures that maintain quality in education and academic freedom in this country's colleges and universities. It defines fundamental professional values and standards for higher education, advances the rights of academics, particularly as those rights pertain to academic freedom and shared governance, and promotes the interests of higher education teaching and research.

American Association of University Women (AAUW)

1310 L Street NW, Suite 1000
Washington, DC 20005
(800) 326-2289
email: connect@aauw.org
website: www.aauw.org

AAUW has been empowering women as individuals and as a community since 1881. It works as a national grassroots organization to improve the lives of millions of women and their families. It conducts research into gender equity issues in education and in the workplace and advocates for policies that improve the lives of girls and women. It also supports challenges to discrimination of women in education and the workplace.

American Civil Liberties Union (ACLU)

125 Broad Street
New York, NY 10004-2400
(212) 549-2500
website: www.aclu.org

The ACLU considers itself to be the nation's guardian of liberty, working in courts, legislatures, and communities to defend and preserve the individual rights and liberties that the Constitution and the laws of the United States guarantee. Among the issues it focuses on are free speech and racial justice.

American Enterprise Institute for Public Policy Research (AEI)

1789 Massachusetts Avenue NW
Washington, DC 20036
(202) 862-5800
email: tyler.castle@aei.org
website: www.aei.org

The American Enterprise Institute is a conservative public policy think tank that sponsors original research on the world economy, US foreign policy and international security, and domestic political and social issues. AEI is dedicated to defending human dignity, expanding human potential, and building a freer and safer world.

Anti-Defamation League (ADL)

605 Third Avenue
New York, NY 10158
(212) 885-7970
email: newyork@adl.com
website: www.adl.org

Founded in 1913, the Anti-Defamation League is a US civil rights/ human relations organization. It has a history of reminding the world just how tenuous civil rights are and it mobilizes people to engage in reasonable discourse as together we find solutions to serve our diverse society.

Cato Institute
1000 Massachusetts Avenue NW
Washington, DC 20001-5403
(202) 842-0200
website: www.cato.org

The Cato Institute is a libertarian public policy research organization, a think tank dedicated to the principles of individual liberty, limited government, free markets, and peace. Its scholars and analysts conduct independent research on a wide range of policy issues.

National Education Association (NEA)
1201 16th Street NW
Washington, DC 20036-3290
(202) 833-4000
website: www.nea.org

The National Education Association is America's largest teachers' organization. The NEA is committed to advancing the cause of public education. The NEA has affiliate organizations in every state and in more than 14,000 communities across the United States. It works to ensure that every student receives a quality education.

National Women's Law Center (NWLC)
11 Dupont Circle NW, #800
Washington, DC 20036
(202) 588-5180
website: www. nwlc.org

The National Women's Law Center fights for gender justice in court, in public policy, and in society. It focuses on issues that are central to the lives of women and girls. It uses legal means to change culture and drive solutions to the gender inequity that shapes our society and to break down barriers. It especially aids those who face multiple forms of discrimination, including women of color, LGBTQ people, and low-income women and families.

US Commission on Civil Rights (USCCR)

1331 Pennsylvania Avenue NW, Suite 1150
Washington, DC 20425
(202) 376-7700
website: www.usccr.gov

Established as an independent, bipartisan, fact-finding government agency, the USCCR's mission is to inform the development of national civil rights policy and enhance enforcement of federal civil rights laws. It pursues this mission by studying alleged deprivations of voting rights and alleged discrimination based on race, color, religion, sex, age, disability, or national origin, or in the administration of justice.

Bibliography of Books

Cara Acred. *Censorship*. Cambridge, UK: Independence, 2015.

John Allen. *Cancel Culture: Social Justice or Mob Rule?* San Diego, CA: Referencepoint Press, 2022.

Dorothy A. Brown. *Critical Race Theory: Cases, Materials, and Problems*. St. Paul, MN: West Academic Publishing, 2014.

Richard Delgado. *Critical Race Theory: The Cutting Edge*. Philadelphia, PA: Temple University Press, 2013.

Alan Dershowitz. *Cancel Culture: The Latest Attack on Free Speech and Due Process*. New York, NY: Hot Books, 2020.

Alan Dershowitz. *Case Against the New Censorship: Protecting Free Speech from Big Tech, Progressives, and Universities*. New York, NY: Hot Books, 2021.

Adrienne D. Dixson. *Critical Race Theory in Education*. London, UK: Routledge, 2018.

Kevin Donnelly. *Cancel Culture and the Left's Long March*. Melbourne, Australia: Wilkinson Publishing, 2021.

Paul du Quenoy. *Cancel Culture: Tales from the Front Lines*. Washington, DC: Academica Press, 2021.

Mary Grabar. *Debunking the 1619 Project: Exposing the Plan to Divide America*. Washington, DC: Regnery History, 2021.

Ryan Hartwig. *Behind the Mask of Facebook: A Whistleblower's Shocking Story of Big Tech Bias and Censorship*. New York, NY: W. W. Norton, 2021.

Dan Kovalik. *Cancel This Book: The Progressive Case Against Cancel Culture*. New York, NY: Hot Books, 2021.

Greg Lukianoff. *Unlearning Liberty: Campus Censorship and the End of American Debate*. New York, NY: Encounter Books, 2014. Phillip W. Magness. *The 1619 Project: A Critique*.

Great Barrington, MA: American Institute for Economic Research, 2020.

Joel Simon. *The New Censorship: Inside the Global Battle for Media Freedom*. New York, NY: Columbia University Press, 2019.

Lita Sorensen, ed. *Cancel Culture*. New York, NY: Greenhaven Publishing, 2021.

Stephen E. Strang. *God and Cancel Culture: Stand Strong Before It's Too Late*. Brandon, FL: Frontline, 2021.

Index